FAMILY STYLE

SHARED PLATES FOR CASUAL FEASTS

FAMILY

STYLE

KAREN TEDESCO

CREATOR OF FAMILYSTYLE FOOD

PAGE STREET
PUBLISHING CO.

PAGE STREET
PUBLISHING CO.

Copyright © 2020 Karen Tedesco

First published in 2020 by
Page Street Publishing Co.
27 Congress Street, Suite 105
Salem, MA 01970
www.pagestreetpublishing.com

Distributed by Macmillan, sales in Canada by The Canadian Manda Group.

24 23 22 21 20   1 2 3 4 5

ISBN-13: 978-1-64567-116-9
ISBN-10: 1-64567-116-X

Library of Congress Control Number: 2019957311

Cover and book design by Molly Gillespie for Page Street Publishing Co.
Photography by Karen Tedesco

Printed and bound in China

For my parents and grandparents,
who taught me how to eat family style.

CONTENTS

INTRODUCTION

Cooking isn't just a means to an end—it's an everyday act that bonds us together.

Family Style is all about sharing delicious, home-cooked food with people you care about. The goal is to inspire you to take a relaxed approach to cooking for a group. Think abundant plates of Sunday-style pasta sauced with a rich pork ragu (page 91); spiced, roasted carrots generously heaped onto a platter (page 143); and an oversized bowl that holds a flavor-packed chickpea salad with tangy tahini sauce (page 33).

Gathering around a table—whether that "table" happens to be your kitchen island, your coffee table or just a blanket spread on the grass—is an elemental way for people to connect. No matter what else is happening in the world, sitting down together to share a meal is a mutually rewarding experience.

I know—it all sounds like something to aspire to. So let's agree that keeping things uncomplicated is equally important.

When I cook, I don't want to use lots of pots, pans and dishes that need cleaning up, so my recipes are generally streamlined and easy to pull off, even on a weeknight.

Nor do I expect you to have to search high and low for ingredients to make a recipe. Although my own pantry is stocked with all kinds of oils, spices and seasonings—the "goodies" that inspire me as a creative cook— I've based this recipe collection on ingredients you can buy at any well-stocked grocery store and at your local farmers' market.

A LITTLE ABOUT ME

My entire career has revolved around food. I started as a server in restaurants before making my way into the kitchen, where I began to cook professionally and, later, as a personal chef.

Eventually, my creative impulse led me to food photography and recipe development, where I found my happy place: working on my blog Familystyle Food. It's my dream job! I'm always thinking about new recipes, jotting down ideas and imagining the best way to capture the qualities of a beautiful plate with my camera.

All the while, I'm in constant pursuit of the secret to unlocking flavor in food, truly an intangible element. There isn't a word in the English language that can describe the feeling you get after a bite of something so tasty you literally hum with pleasure: Mmmmm. But that's exactly what I aim to bring out with every recipe I create. (Yes, I set that bar pretty high.)

I'm always searching for flavors that wake up my senses.

But it has to be simple.

I had a bowl of soup in Italy that was life changing. It was just tomato soup—pappa al pomodoro—a Tuscan classic made with ripe summer tomatoes, bread and olive oil. How did so few ingredients taste like the sweet essence of summer, feel like warm sunshine on my skin and sound like olive leaves rustling in the breeze? It was only soup, but it was transportive—and all I needed to do was savor it.

That's what I mean by simple: taking a few things—a fruit or vegetable, a few glugs of olive oil and a sprinkle of flaky sea salt—and putting them together so they become something much more than a sum of their parts.

We all love to eat food that makes us swoon with happiness inside. I'd like to help you find nourishment in the process of preparing and sharing it as well.

WHAT YOU'LL FIND IN THIS BOOK

Next to simplicity, the secret to keeping up a regular rhythm of home cooking lies in creating a core collection of dishes—the ones that delight the taste buds, the ones you make over and over without getting bored with them.

My recipes don't adhere to any particular dietary restrictions, but they do revolve around good-quality, minimally processed pantry ingredients and seasonal produce. I strongly believe that a varied diet that includes a little bit of everything, along with a lot of vegetables, is a crucial component of a healthy, exuberant life.

In the true spirit of family-style eating, the dishes in this book are designed to complement each other. *Family Style* contains 60 recipes that are meant to be flexibly combined for everyday feasting: Match the most delicious, crisp-skinned chicken (page 55) with crusty Parmesan potatoes (page 135) and one of my flavor-packed vegetable salads for a delicious casual dinner.

That's the beauty of putting an assortment of food on the table to share: It allows everyone to choose their own adventure. Plus, the act of sharing and passing platters around the table gets people engaged and puts them at ease. Most of these recipes are accompanied by "For a Family-Style Feast" suggestions for dishes to mix and match.

And because everyone loves an occasional sweet treat, I'm sharing a chapter with a handful of my favorites, which include—truly—the best chewy chocolate chip cookies (page 148) and my most requested recipe for moist, lemony cornmeal cake (page 155).

I hope this book will find a comfortable place in your kitchen, providing you with a blueprint of recipes that will encourage you to cook more at home, to eat well and to invite friends and family over to share it all with.

Karen

A NOTE ON SALT

Salt is the key to unlocking flavor in your cooking. I use two kinds of salt in this book—kosher salt and flaked sea salt, such as Maldon.

I've gotten into the habit of specifying an exact amount of salt when I write recipes, rather than saying "salt to taste," because honestly, I've learned that people are afraid to use enough salt. The amount of salt called for in these recipes serves as a benchmark, but absolutely adjust to suit your personal preference.

Because granules of kosher salt are fluffier than table salt, there's less salt per volume in a teaspoon of kosher salt than there is in fine salt. My preferred brand of kosher salt is Diamond, and it's what I used to test all the recipes in this book.

If you use a brand of kosher salt other than Diamond, such as Morton, reduce the amount of salt specified by one-half (because it's twice as salty).

BITES AND SALADS
TO SHARE

WHEN I WALK INTO MY KITCHEN TO MAKE DINNER, two things usually happen. First, I find a great playlist and turn on music and, second, I pour myself a glass of wine. It doesn't matter if I'm about to cook for the family, for a gathering of friends or just for myself: Setting the mood creates an atmosphere of active anticipation and the best kind of hunger.

I wanted to begin this book the same way I approach cooking a meal at my house: with recipes for dishes that will wake up your taste buds. If you start out with a casual vibe and a piqued appetite, you'll find your appetite only increases as you get into a cooking groove. I always find the tactile experience of cooking deliciously sensual. Once you start chopping vegetables, dipping your finger into the dressing for a taste check and finally tossing the ingredients on the cutting board into a big salad bowl, you can't wait to sit down and just dig in.

This chapter includes recipes for vibrant fare designed to get people salivating, dishes that can either kick-start a meal or sit on the table alongside heartier ones, like crunchy, sweet-and-salty Rosemary and Fennel Roasted Almonds (page 14), Super Creamy Homemade Hummus (page 17) and Black Bean Tostadas with Avocado Mash (page 18). My hearty, flavor-packed salads can just as easily serve as a main event or as a collection of sides that make a meal—like Kale Caesar Salad with Olive Oil Breadcrumbs (page 25) and Falafel-Spiced Chickpea Salad (page 33).

ROSEMARY AND FENNEL ROASTED ALMONDS

1 egg white (2 tbsp [30 ml])

1 tbsp (15 g) brown sugar

1 tbsp (3 g) chopped fresh rosemary

1 tsp ground fennel seed

1 tsp sea salt

½ tsp freshly ground black pepper

2½ cups (355 g) whole almonds

Flaky sea salt, such as Maldon

I remember being a kid, always trying to weasel my way into the room when my parents were entertaining people bigger than me. There would always be simple snacks on the table: uncomplicated things like pretzels, chips and salted nuts—the things everyone likes to munch on that also happen to go well with adult beverages. These roasted almonds are my version of a grown-up party snack, although once you try them, it's easy to find yourself sneaking handfuls all day long. I pack them into containers and throw them into my bag whenever I head out for the day. A coating of egg white, spices and aromatic herbs gives them a sweet-saltiness to crave. Don't skip the final sprinkle of flaky salt—and pour some very cold prosecco to wash them down.

MAKES 2½ CUPS [355 G]

Preheat the oven to 300°F (150°C). Line a large rimmed baking sheet with a piece of parchment paper.

Whisk the egg white, brown sugar, rosemary, fennel, salt and pepper in a large bowl until the mixture is combined. Stir in the almonds.

Dump the almonds onto the baking sheet, spreading them out in one layer. Bake them for 25 minutes, until the almonds are golden. Remove the almonds from the oven and cool them completely, about 25 minutes—they will crisp up more as they cool. Sprinkle with the flaky salt and serve.

SUPER CREAMY
HOMEMADE HUMMUS

2 (15-oz [425-g]) cans chickpeas, drained (reserve ½ cup [120 ml] liquid)

2 cloves garlic, sliced

2 tbsp (30 ml) extra virgin olive oil, plus more for garnish

1½ tsp (5 g) kosher salt

½ cup (110 g) tahini

¼ cup (60 ml) fresh lemon juice (from approximately 2 lemons)

Smoked paprika, optional

You know when a certain food sinks its hooks into you and won't let go? That's what hummus did to me years and years ago, when I decided it would be a good idea to become a vegetarian (it wasn't). Back then, there weren't many plant-based options for a college student aside from lentils, raw carrots and, well . . . hummus. But somehow, I've never grown tired of it. This is my homemade version, and it's so worth making. Yes, you can buy a plastic tub of hummus anywhere, including gas station quick marts, but come on! It will never compare to this ultrasmooth version that you can whip up yourself. The secret to its luscious texture is simple: Cook the canned chickpeas with garlic and olive oil before you process them, which will soften and season them inside and out.

MAKES ABOUT 4½ CUPS [1 KG]

Put the chickpeas, reserved liquid, garlic and the 2 tablespoons (30 ml) of olive oil in a medium saucepan over medium heat. When the mixture starts to simmer, lower the heat and cook for 10 minutes, partially covered. Let the mixture cool to room temperature, about 15 minutes.

Transfer the chickpeas and the liquid to a food processor. Add the salt, tahini and lemon juice and process for 2 to 3 minutes, until the mixture is very smooth, light and creamy.

Transfer the hummus to a shallow bowl or plate, and smooth it out with the back of a spoon. Drizzle the hummus with more olive oil to taste and sprinkle it with the smoked paprika to garnish, if you like.

The hummus will keep, refrigerated, for up to a week.

FOR A FAMILY-STYLE FEAST

I can think of no better feast than a Mediterranean-style nosh. This hummus brings it all together—it goes perfectly with a platter of Roasted Mediterranean Vegetables (page 131), Baked Harissa Chicken Thighs with Chickpeas (page 56) and Charred Broccoli Salad (page 29).

BLACK BEAN TOSTADAS WITH AVOCADO MASH

TOSTADAS

2 tbsp (30 ml) extra virgin olive oil, plus more for baking the tortillas

½ cup (70 g) chopped red onion

1 tsp finely chopped or grated garlic

2 tsp (6 g) chili powder

1 (15-oz [425-g]) can black beans, drained

1 tbsp (15 ml) hot sauce (I like Cholula)

2 tbsp (30 ml) water

2 avocados, pitted and peeled

3 tbsp (45 ml) fresh lime juice

Kosher salt, to taste

6 corn tortillas

TOPPINGS

1 cup (120 g) crumbled feta cheese

Soft lettuce leaves, such as Boston, torn or sliced

Fresh cilantro leaves

Sliced green onions

Okay, so this is basically chips and guac, but it's next-level chips and guac. Start with good corn tortillas, crisp them up in the oven and top them off with spiced-up black beans and your favorite taco garnishes.

SERVES 4–6

For the tostadas, preheat the oven to 425°F (220°C).

Heat the olive oil in a medium skillet over medium-high heat. Add the onion and cook until it's softened, about 5 minutes. Stir in the garlic and chili powder and cook for about 30 seconds, until fragrant. Stir in the black beans, hot sauce and water. Cover the pan and simmer the beans for 10 minutes.

Meanwhile, in a bowl, mash the avocados to a creamy but chunky texture with the lime juice and salt.

Brush the tortillas lightly with olive oil and arrange them on a rimmed baking sheet in one layer. Bake the tortillas for 5 minutes, then flip them over and bake for another 5 minutes, until they are crisp.

To serve, spread some of the black bean mixture on each tostada and spoon a nice blob of the mashed avocado over it.

For the toppings, sprinkle the tostadas with the feta cheese, lettuce, cilantro and green onions.

FOR A FAMILY-STYLE FEAST

Go with the theme of a Mexican-style celebration and serve the tostadas with Beer-Braised Pulled Pork (page 87), Chicken Posole Verde (page 125) and plenty of cold beer.

POTATO AND GOAT CHEESE FLATBREAD

1 (14-oz [397-g]) sheet frozen puff pastry dough, thawed according to package directions (keep it cold until ready to use)

2 tbsp (30 ml) extra virgin olive oil, divided

1 tsp finely chopped or grated garlic

2 tsp (2 g) chopped fresh thyme or rosemary

8 oz (230 g) baby Yukon Gold potatoes, unpeeled and cut into parchment paper–thin slices

Flaky sea salt, such as Maldon

Freshly ground black pepper

2 green onions, sliced

¼ cup (8 g) freshly grated Parmesan cheese

½ cup (56 g) crumbled goat cheese

2 tbsp (30 g) Walnut-Parsley Pesto (page 108) or prepared pesto sauce

2 cups (40 g) baby arugula greens

This is my quick take on a white pizza—*pizza bianca*—a savory tart topped with potatoes, cheese, pesto and arugula greens. The secret to making it is to use frozen puff pastry dough instead of a traditional yeasted pizza dough. I love how the thinly sliced potatoes (I use a mandoline to slice them) turn out tender with crisp edges, merging into the flaky pastry and soft goat cheese . . . it's a carb lover's dream. I recommend using an all-butter puff pastry dough—Dufour has a good and readily available one.

SERVES 14-16

Preheat the oven to 425°F (220°C). Line a large rimmed baking sheet with parchment paper.

Place the pastry dough on the prepared sheet and unfold it. Using your hands, press the dough into a rustic rectangular shape that almost reaches the edges of the pan—don't worry if it's not perfect. Poke random holes all around the dough with a fork or a small, sharp knife.

Drizzle the dough with 1 tablespoon (15 ml) of the olive oil and sprinkle it with the garlic and thyme, rubbing them evenly over the surface.

Toss the potatoes in a bowl with the remaining 1 tablespoon (15 ml) of olive oil, and season them with salt and pepper to taste.

Layer the potato slices over the dough, overlapping them and leaving a ½-inch (12-mm) border around the edges. Scatter the green onions over the potatoes and sprinkle them with the Parmesan.

Bake the flatbread until the edges of the crust are puffed and golden, 17 to 20 minutes.

Remove the flatbread from the oven and immediately top it with the goat cheese. Spoon the pesto randomly over the flatbread, then sprinkle it with the arugula. Slice into pieces with a knife or pizza cutter to serve.

FOR A FAMILY-STYLE FEAST

Find an excuse to throw a weekend lunch or brunch and serve this flatbread along with two or three of the salads in this chapter; they are all great to serve at room temperature. Don't forget bottles of chilled prosecco!

ROASTED ZA'ATAR CAULIFLOWER SALAD

1 head cauliflower (about 2 lbs [910 g]), cut into bite-size pieces

¼ cup (60 ml) extra virgin olive oil, plus more for serving

1½ tsp (5 g) kosher salt

2 tsp (4 g) za'atar

1 tsp ground cumin

½ tsp crushed red pepper

1 (15-oz [425-g]) can chickpeas, drained

1 clove garlic, finely sliced

1 lemon

⅓ cup (40 g) crumbled feta cheese

3–4 cups (60–80 g) sturdy baby greens, such as kale, spinach or arugula

Flaky sea salt, such as Maldon

Cauliflower is a vegetable I find hard to resist, but especially so when it's roasted. Roasted cauliflower hardly needs anything but olive oil and salt to make it taste nutty and delicious. But spicing it up with the pungent herb blend za'atar makes it extra special. Toss the warm roasted florets with feta cheese, tender leafy greens and the juice of a lemon to add sparky brightness. An otherwise plain pan of roasted vegetables becomes a hearty meal salad or side dish. Za'atar is a Middle Eastern spice blend of dried wild thyme, sumac and sesame seeds. It's terrific sprinkled on anything, from hummus to avocado toast.

SERVES 4–6

Preheat the oven to 425°F (220°C).

Spread the cauliflower on a rimmed baking sheet in one layer. Drizzle it with the ¼ cup (60 ml) of oil. Sprinkle the salt, za'atar, cumin and crushed red pepper evenly over the cauliflower, then toss everything to coat it with the spices.

Roast the cauliflower for 20 minutes. Add the chickpeas and garlic to the pan and stir them around. Return the pan to the oven and roast for 10 to 12 more minutes, until the cauliflower is tender and golden brown.

Use a rasp grater, such as a microplane, to zest the lemon over the cauliflower. Slice the lemon in half and squeeze the juice of both halves over everything. Sprinkle the feta cheese and greens over the cauliflower and toss gently to combine the ingredients.

Transfer the mixture to a large serving bowl or platter. Drizzle with more oil to taste, and add a pinch or two of the flaky salt. Serve the salad warm or at room temperature.

FOR A FAMILY-STYLE FEAST

Reimagine dinner, vegetarian style. Serve this hearty salad with Rigatoni with Walnut-Parsley Pesto (page 108), Garlicky Greens with Olive Oil (page 128) and Roasted Mediterranean Vegetables (page 131).

KALE CAESAR SALAD WITH OLIVE OIL BREADCRUMBS

SALAD

14–16 oz (400–455 g) Tuscan (lacinato) kale (2 bunches)

3 slices good, crusty sourdough bread, cut into cubes

2 tbsp (30 ml) extra virgin olive oil

2-oz (55-g) chunk ricotta salata cheese (or substitute Pecorino Toscano or Romano)

TAHINI CAESAR DRESSING

¼ cup (60 ml) fresh lemon juice

¼ cup (55 g) tahini

¼ cup (60 ml) extra virgin olive oil

3–4 tbsp (45–60 ml) cold water

1 clove garlic, chopped

3 tbsp (6 g) freshly grated Pecorino Romano or Parmesan cheese

½ tsp crushed red pepper

½ tsp sea salt

Kale salad outgrew its trendy moment and now it's a classic. Say what you will about kale (haters gonna hate), but it will always have a place in my heart. The sturdy, dark-green leaves practically beg to be paired with a zesty, lemony dressing. Unlike a classic Caesar dressing, this one is made with tahini instead of an eggy mayo base. And rather than croutons, I top the salad with toasty breadcrumbs, which provide a downright addictive crunch. Kale leaves are sturdy, so if you dress the salad an hour or so before serving, it will hold up well, but add the breadcrumbs at the last minute so they don't get soggy. The dressing will keep for up to three days in the fridge; whisk in a tablespoon (15 ml) or so of water if it becomes too thick.

SERVES 4-6

For the salad, trim off the bases of the kale bunches and remove the ribs from each leaf—you can either tear them out by zipping your fingers lengthwise along the stem, or use a knife if it's easier. Stack the leaves and slice the kale into ribbons. Wash and dry the kale in a salad spinner, then transfer it to a large serving bowl.

Put the bread cubes in a blender or food processor and pulse until you have about 1 cup (50 g) of coarse crumbs.

Place a 10- to 12-inch (25- to 31-cm) skillet over medium heat. When the pan is hot, add the oil and the breadcrumbs. Cook for about 5 minutes, stirring once or twice, until the crumbs crisp up and smell toasty. Remove the pan from the heat.

To make the dressing, combine the lemon juice, tahini, oil, water, garlic, Pecorino, crushed red pepper and salt in a blender or food processor until the mixture is very smooth.

Pour half of the dressing over the kale leaves, and toss to coat them. Sprinkle the kale with the breadcrumbs and toss again. Grate the ricotta salata cheese over the salad, and serve it with extra dressing on the side.

CHILI-GARLIC CUCUMBER SALAD WITH SESAME

3 tbsp (45 ml) avocado or canola oil

2 cloves garlic, grated on a microplane or finely chopped

½–1 tsp crushed red pepper, to taste

6 Persian cucumbers (1½ lbs [680 g]), sliced into 1-inch (2.5-cm) half-moons

1 tsp kosher salt

1 tsp brown sesame seeds

½ cup (15 g) torn fresh mint or (6 g) cilantro leaves (or a combination)

2 tsp (10 ml) rice vinegar

1 tbsp (15 ml) fresh lime juice

3 tbsp (30 g) chopped unsalted roasted peanuts

Cooling, refreshing cucumbers are so, so good paired with the contrasting flavor-bomb of garlic and spicy chili. It's almost as though they were born to be together. Briefly heating the garlic and crushed red pepper, or chili flakes, in oil tamps down the pungency of the raw garlic, creating a tasty, infused oil to dress the salad. A full teaspoon of chili flakes makes a spicy oil that I happen to love, but feel free to adjust the amount to suit your taste.

SERVES 4

Place the oil, garlic and crushed red pepper in a small saucepan over medium heat. Remove the pan from the heat as soon as the garlic is fragrant and sizzling, about 2 minutes; be sure not to brown the garlic.

Put the cucumbers in a large bowl. Sprinkle them with the salt, sesame seeds and mint leaves, and toss them gently. Pour the garlic oil over the cucumbers, then sprinkle them with the vinegar, lime juice and peanuts. Toss the salad to combine everything and serve.

FOR A FAMILY-STYLE FEAST

This cooling salad is the perfect partner with bold, spicy dishes. Put it on the table next to the Stir-Fried Pork and Rice Noodle Bowl (page 47) and Thai Basil Chicken (page 59).

CHARRED BROCCOLI SALAD

DRESSING

2 tsp (7 g) finely chopped shallot

1 tsp grated fresh lemon zest

2 tsp (10 ml) fresh lemon juice

1 tsp rice wine or white wine vinegar

1 tsp Dijon mustard

Kosher salt and freshly ground black pepper, to taste

3 tbsp (45 ml) extra virgin olive oil

SALAD

1 bunch broccoli (about 2 lbs [910 g])

3 tbsp (45 ml) extra virgin olive oil

1 tsp kosher salt

1 green onion including green top, sliced

2 tbsp (6 g) chopped fresh Italian parsley

1 tbsp (6 g) pine nuts

A few years ago, I changed things up and started making roasted broccoli the easy way: under the broiler. And it was mind-blowing. You can broil broccoli in a fraction of the time it takes to roast it, and it comes out deliciously, irresistibly charred on the edges. The lemony dressing is good with other roasted vegetables, too. This salad is a good choice to make ahead—it will happily sit at room temperature and get even tastier.

SERVES 4-6

Position the oven rack so that it's 10 or 12 inches (25 or 31 cm) from the heat source, and preheat the broiler to high.

To make the dressing, whisk the shallot, lemon zest and juice, vinegar, mustard, salt and pepper together in a bowl. Slowly drizzle in the oil, while whisking, until the dressing is smooth and emulsified. Taste it and add more salt and pepper, if you like.

For the salad, slice off and discard the tough lower broccoli stalks. Cut the broccoli into bite-size florets. Slice the tender, light green sections of the upper stalk into bite-size pieces.

Put the broccoli pieces on a rimmed baking sheet. Pour the olive oil over the broccoli, sprinkle it with the salt and toss it around to coat.

Slide the baking sheet under the broiler and cook for 5 minutes. Stir the broccoli around and toss in the green onion. Continue broiling for about 5 more minutes, until the pieces are bright green, tender and charred on the edges.

Transfer the broccoli to a serving bowl and stir in the parsley and pine nuts. Drizzle the salad with the dressing, and toss the salad gently. Serve the salad warm or at room temperature.

BLACK LENTIL SALAD WITH SPINACH AND GOAT CHEESE

3 tbsp (45 ml) extra virgin olive oil, divided

1 small shallot, finely chopped (2 tbsp [20 g])

1 cup (200 g) black or French green lentils

¾ tsp kosher salt

2 cups (480 ml) vegetable broth or water

2 tsp (10 ml) red wine vinegar

2 cups (40 g) baby spinach leaves

¼ cup (25 g) thinly sliced red onion

1 Persian or baby cucumber, sliced

Freshly ground black pepper

2 oz (55 g) soft goat cheese

Black lentils—also called beluga lentils, because they look like fancy caviar—are worth seeking out. They taste as earthy and satisfying as everyday brown lentils, only these tiny beauties hold their shape elegantly after they're cooked, making them a great base for an interesting salad. This is one of those recipes you can make for dinner one night and happily take to work for lunch the next day.

SERVES 4-6

Heat 1 tablespoon (15 ml) of the olive oil in a heavy saucepan over medium heat. Add the shallot and cook until it's softened, about 5 minutes.

Stir in the lentils and the salt. Pour in the broth, bring the mixture to a simmer, then reduce the heat and partially cover the pan. Cook for 25 minutes, or until the lentils have absorbed most of the liquid and are cooked through, but are not mushy. Drain any liquid that remains in the pan.

Transfer the lentils to a serving bowl. Add the remaining 2 tablespoons (30 ml) of olive oil, the vinegar, spinach, onion, cucumber and a few grinds of black pepper to taste. Mix gently to combine.

Crumble the goat cheese over the salad and serve.

FALAFEL-SPICED CHICKPEA SALAD

TAHINI SAUCE

⅓ cup (73 g) tahini

⅓ cup (80 ml) cold water

2 tbsp (30 ml) apple cider vinegar

2 tbsp (30 ml) toasted sesame oil

1 tbsp (15 ml) fresh lemon juice

1 clove garlic, grated on a microplane or finely chopped

2 tsp (4 g) ground cumin

1 tsp smoked paprika

1 tsp hot sauce (I like Cholula)

1 tsp kosher salt

¼ tsp cayenne pepper

SALAD

½ cup (50 g) thinly sliced red onion

2 romaine lettuce hearts, washed and trimmed

2 Persian or baby cucumbers, sliced into rounds

1 (15-oz [425-g]) can (or 2 cups [330 g] cooked) chickpeas, drained

2 cups (488 g) cherry tomatoes, halved

½ cup (6 g) fresh cilantro or (15 g) mint leaves (or a mixture)

½ cup (60 g) crumbled feta cheese

1 (6-inch [15-cm]) pita bread, toasted and cut into triangles

I'm crazy about falafel and have been known to stalk certain NYC food carts for an occasional fix. But let's face it: It can be a project to make at home (all that deep-frying!). Also, let's admit that falafel can be very filling, which is good when you're not planning to eat for the rest of the day, but not so good if you want to feel nourished but not brutally stuffed. This recipe is my way to combine all the flavors I crave into one big, satisfying salad that feels just right. Make it for lunch, or turn it into a more substantial meal by pairing it with cooked shrimp, salmon or chicken.

SERVES 4–6

To make the sauce, put the tahini, water, vinegar, oil, lemon juice, garlic, cumin, paprika, hot sauce, salt and cayenne in a blender or small food processor, and process until the mixture is very smooth and creamy.

For the salad, place the red onion slices in a small bowl and cover them with cold water. Soak the onions for 10 minutes, then drain and pat them dry with a clean towel—this will mellow the onion's sharpness.

To assemble the salad, tear any large romaine leaves into pieces. Layer one half of the leaves in a large serving bowl. Top with half of each of the onion, cucumbers, chickpeas, tomatoes, cilantro and feta. Drizzle with ¼ cup (60 ml) of the Tahini Sauce.

Repeat the layering with the remaining ingredients and drizzle more sauce to taste over the top.

Toss the salad just before serving, and arrange the pita slices around the edge of the bowl. Serve additional Tahini Sauce on the side.

FOR A FAMILY-STYLE FEAST

Because it holds up well at room temperature, this is a salad that begs to be brought outside with Super Creamy Homemade Hummus (page 17) and Farro and Burrata with Burst Tomatoes (page 122) for a good hang with friends in the backyard.

BIG GREEN SALAD

RED WINE VINAIGRETTE

3 tbsp (45 ml) red wine vinegar

2 tbsp (20 g) chopped shallot

1 clove garlic, grated on a microplane or finely chopped

1 tbsp (15 ml) water

1 tsp kosher salt

¼ tsp freshly ground black pepper

2 tbsp (4 g) freshly grated Parmesan cheese

1 tbsp (15 g) Dijon mustard

2 tsp (10 ml) honey

¾ cup (180 ml) extra virgin olive oil

SALAD

1 head Boston or Bibb lettuce

2 romaine lettuce hearts

3 heads Little Gem lettuce

4 cups (80 g) baby arugula leaves

½ cup (6 g) fresh Italian parsley leaves

1 green onion including green top, chopped

Flaky sea salt, such as Maldon

¼ cup (30 g) Marcona almonds, coarsely chopped

Welcome to the simplest, most mouthwatering salad. When I was growing up, a classic iceberg salad was the norm, but that was back in the day before fancy baby greens came in plastic boxes. Nothing against those, but there's something wonderful about making a green salad with old-fashioned head lettuce. You get a shareable bowlful of green leaves that yield a variety of textures: sweet, tender leaves of Boston lettuce that contrast with the refreshing crunch of romaine, nutty arugula and an herby hit of parsley leaves. The salad is tossed with a tangy-sweet dressing that could become your new house favorite. It goes with just about everything in this book.

SERVES 4

To make the dressing, put the vinegar, shallot, garlic, water and salt in a medium bowl. Let the mixture macerate for 5 minutes, then add the pepper, cheese, Dijon and honey. Whisk the dressing, while slowly pouring in the oil, until the dressing is smooth and emulsified. The dressing can be made up to three days ahead and stored in the refrigerator—shake it up before using it.

For the salad, separate the leaves from the Boston, romaine and Little Gem lettuces, trimming off any wilted or discolored ones. Wash and dry the lettuce in a salad spinner and pat it with a clean, dry towel to absorb any excess water. Tear any large leaves in half.

Put all the lettuce leaves in a large salad bowl, along with the arugula, parsley and green onion. Sprinkle with a pinch of flaky salt, and drizzle the salad with a generous amount of the dressing. Toss gently, then taste a leaf, adding a bit more dressing to taste.

Sprinkle the salad with the almonds and serve.

NOTE: Little Gem is a type of lettuce that's like a cross between romaine and butter lettuce—if you can't find it, just use a bit extra of the Boston lettuce and romaine hearts.

MEATY
MAINS

MEATS LIKE PORK, BEEF, LAMB AND CHICKEN are at the heart of many a meal, so much so that they're often considered the main event. This chapter offers recipes to satisfy non-vegetarians. Although my omnivorous approach to cooking and eating has grown less meat-centered, I do enjoy it on my plate several times a week, along with a large platter of vegetables or a hearty salad. To me it feels like a well-rounded way to enjoy food.

There isn't a dish that's cozier than Herby Spatchcock Chicken (page 55), and I've worked hard to perfect a method that yields juicy perfection with the chicken seasoned inside and out and with all parts cooked to just the right degree of doneness.

Thai Basil Chicken (page 59) is a mainstay on time-strapped nights—like something you'd crave for takeout, only much better. And it's just as quick from start to finish.

When it comes to beef, I'm sharing my method for preparing my favorite cut: The Best Steak Is a Skirt Steak (page 48). And I hope you'll be tempted to make my lamb sliders (page 52); they're so tasty I tear up with happiness every time I eat them. If you never consider cooking with lamb, these burgers will change your mind.

All the recipes serve four to six people and will go even further as part of a feast with any of the salads from the previous chapter (Bites and Salads to Share, page 12) and any dishes from the Vegetables by the Platter chapter (page 126).

MOM'S CLASSIC ITALIAN MEATBALLS WITH SIMPLE RED SAUCE

SIMPLE RED SAUCE

2 tbsp (30 ml) extra virgin olive oil

½ cup (70 g) finely chopped yellow onion

2 tbsp (28 g) finely chopped or grated garlic

1 (28-oz [794-g]) can whole peeled tomatoes or crushed tomatoes

1 (24-oz [680-g]) jar tomato passata or purée

1–2 tsp (4–7 g) kosher salt

Freshly ground black pepper, to taste

1 tsp sugar

My mom made the best meatballs, and everyone in our family knew it. After she died, I made hundreds of meatballs before I finally got close to nailing her recipe. It turns out the secret to perfect meatballs lies in the milk-soaked fresh breadcrumbs, which keep the meat from drying out. This is the one recipe you need for tender, tasty and downright juicy meatballs that beg to be sauced with my easiest, most delicious quick-cooking red sauce.

MAKES ABOUT 16 MEATBALLS

To make the sauce, put the oil and onion in a large saucepan, and place it over medium heat. Cook and stir until the onion is softened, about 5 minutes. Stir in the garlic and cook for a minute, until it smells fragrant.

Add the tomatoes, tomato passata, salt to taste, pepper and the sugar to the pot.

Bring the sauce to a simmer, using a wooden spoon to break the tomatoes into smaller pieces, or use an immersion blender for a smoother texture, if you prefer.

Cook the sauce for 20 minutes. Taste for seasoning and keep it warm. The sauce will keep, refrigerated, for 5 days, or frozen, for 1 month.

(continued)

MEATBALLS

½ cup (42 g) fresh breadcrumbs
(see Note)

¼ cup (60 ml) milk

2 egg yolks

½ cup (16 g) freshly grated
Pecorino Romano cheese

1 tbsp (10 g) kosher salt or
1½ tsp (10 g) table salt (see note
on salt, page 11)

1 tsp freshly ground black
pepper

2 cloves garlic, grated on a
microplane or finely chopped

1 lb (455 g) ground beef chuck

1 lb (455 g) ground pork

⅓ cup (60 g) grated yellow or
white onion

½ cup (6 g) fresh Italian parsley
or basil (or a mixture of both),
roughly chopped

Extra virgin olive oil

For the meatballs, put the breadcrumbs in a large bowl. Pour the milk over the crumbs and stir to coat the crumbs. Mix in the egg yolks, cheese, salt, pepper and garlic until the ingredients are combined.

Add the beef, pork, onion and parsley. Blend everything together well, using your hands or a large wooden spoon. You can also use a standing mixer fitted with the paddle attachment. Mix for 1 to 2 minutes, just until the mixture looks blended.

Use a ¼-cup (60-ml) measuring cup or cookie scoop to portion the meat, then roll the portions into balls. They don't have to be perfect—craggy meatballs have character and hold the sauce better.

Pour enough oil into a large skillet to coat the bottom, and place the pan over medium-high heat. When the pan is hot, add as many meatballs as will fit in the pan without crowding. They should sizzle as soon as they hit the pan; if they don't, the pan isn't hot enough.

Cook the meatballs for 5 to 7 minutes per side, until they're evenly browned. If your pan doesn't fit them all, brown them in two batches.

Finish cooking the meatballs by transferring them to a large saucepan with the red sauce. Simmer the meatballs for 20 to 25 minutes, until they're cooked through. (The meatballs can be made ahead and frozen for up to 2 months.)

NOTE: To make fresh breadcrumbs, trim off the crust from a few slices of hearty country bread. Tear the bread into large pieces and pulse them in a food processor to make coarse pea-sized crumbs.

FOR A FAMILY-STYLE FEAST

This recipe is the ultimate comforting family-style supper. Pour some vino, invite everyone to the table and serve the saucy meatballs with Baked Shells with Ricotta and Greens (page 96) right next to a Big Green Salad (page 34).

STOVETOP PAELLA WITH CHICKEN, CHORIZO AND SHRIMP

SHRIMP BROTH

Shells from 1 lb (455 g) peeled jumbo shrimp

1 small fennel bulb (stalks trimmed) or 3 celery stalks, chopped

1 yellow onion, cut into thick slices

2 carrots, chopped

4 whole cloves garlic

1 bay leaf

1 tsp kosher salt

½ tsp whole black peppercorns

6 cups (1.4 L) water

PAELLA

¼ cup (60 ml) extra virgin olive oil, divided

1½ lbs (680 g) boneless, skinless chicken thighs, cut into 2-inch (5-cm) pieces

¾ lb (340 g) uncooked chorizo sausage, removed from casings

2½ tsp (11 g) kosher salt, divided

1 large yellow onion, chopped

1 red bell pepper, seeded and chopped

2 tbsp (28 g) chopped garlic

Paella could be the ultimate one-pot meal, were it not for the fact that the traditional preparation is actually kind of a big production. But it's so good. I set out to create a doable weeknight version, and this recipe is the happy result. There's something in the pan for everyone: creamy rice, tender chunks of chicken, smoky spiced sausage and shrimp. Pull out your largest skillet for this, ideally one with at least 3-inch (8-cm) sides.

SERVES 6

For the shrimp broth, in a large pot combine the shells, fennel, onion, carrots, garlic, bay leaf, salt, peppercorns and water. Bring the mixture to a boil. Lower the heat and simmer the mixture for 30 minutes, uncovered. Pour the broth through a mesh strainer or colander into a saucepan or large bowl and keep it warm.

For the paella, heat a 14- to 16-inch (36- to 41-cm) paella pan or a large (12- to 14-inch [31- to 36-cm]) pan that has at least 3-inch (8-cm) sides over medium-high heat.

Add 1 tablespoon (15 ml) of the oil, the chicken and chorizo and cook until the chorizo is browned and the exterior of the chicken is opaque, about 10 minutes total (do this in two batches if your pan is less than 14 inches [36 cm] in diameter). Sprinkle the meat with 1 teaspoon of salt, then remove it to a plate, using tongs.

Add the remaining 3 tablespoons (45 ml) of olive oil, the onion, bell pepper and garlic to the pan. Cook, stirring, until the vegetables are softened, about 5 minutes.

(continued)

2 tbsp (30 g) tomato paste

2 tsp (4 g) smoked paprika

½ tsp freshly ground black pepper

¼ tsp cayenne pepper

2 cups (400 g) Spanish bomba rice or Arborio rice

4½ cups (1 L) Shrimp Broth (or substitute with store-bought chicken broth)

1 lb (455 g) jumbo shrimp, peeled (use the shells to make the Shrimp Broth)

⅓ cup (4 g) fresh cilantro or Italian parsley leaves

½ lemon

Add the tomato paste, paprika, black pepper and cayenne to the pan, and stir to coat them with the oil. Stir in the rice, reserved chicken and chorizo, 1½ teaspoons (5 g) of salt and the shrimp broth.

Bring the mixture to a lively simmer and cook it for 18 to 20 minutes, uncovered, until the liquid is almost absorbed and the rice grains rise to the surface of the pan.

Arrange the shrimp over the top of the rice, lower the heat to medium-low and cover the pan. Cook until the shrimp turn pink and are cooked through, 7 to 10 minutes, depending on the size of your shrimp.

Sprinkle the cilantro over the paella, squeeze the lemon over it and serve.

FOR A FAMILY-STYLE FEAST

Nothing exudes the spirit of generosity more than a pan full of paella, even this easy weeknight-friendly version. Serve this straight out of the pan, along with side platters of Roasted Mediterranean Vegetables (page 131) and a Big Green Salad (page 34). The Romesco Sauce (page 71) is a creamy, rich complement to the paella.

15-MINUTE ROSEMARY PORK CHOPS

3 tbsp (45 g) light brown sugar

1 tbsp (10 g) kosher salt

1 tbsp (3 g) chopped fresh rosemary

1 tsp freshly ground black pepper

4 bone-in pork chops, preferably 1½ inches (4 cm) thick

1 tbsp (15 ml) extra virgin olive oil

Brown sugar, salt and fresh rosemary make a dry rub that acts like an instant (well, almost) brine for pork chops. Thin, boneless pork chops can easily become overcooked and dry, so look for thick, bone-in chops that are at least 1½ inches (4 cm) thick—you might have to ask the meat counter to cut them for you. I love rib chops on the bone because they have the best flavor and will turn out juicy every time. Mix up the herbs, too. Try seasoning the chops with sturdy aromatic herbs, like fresh thyme or marjoram, in place of the rosemary. A note on salt: If you don't have kosher salt, use half the amount of regular table salt.

SERVES 4

Preheat the oven to 425°F (220°C).

Combine the brown sugar, salt, rosemary and pepper in a small dish. Sprinkle the mixture on both sides of the pork chops and use your fingers to rub it into the meat.

Let the chops sit for 15 to 30 minutes at room temperature, or cover and refrigerate them for up to 24 hours.

Heat a large (12-inch [31-cm]), heavy, ovenproof skillet—cast iron is perfect—over medium-high heat until a drop of water sizzles and evaporates instantly.

Add the oil to the pan, then add the pork chops (leave the dry rub on). Sear until they are nicely brown on one side, about 5 minutes. Flip the chops over and transfer the skillet to the oven.

Roast the chops for 5 to 7 minutes, or until the pork feels firm to the touch. An instant-read thermometer inserted into the center of the chops should read 140 to 145°F (60 to 63°C).

Transfer the pork chops to a cutting board, and let them rest for 5 to 10 minutes before serving.

FOR A FAMILY-STYLE FEAST

Sometimes it's fun to share a date-night in with a few other couples. Invite 'em over! These chops make a deliciously simple centerpiece. Round out the meal with Kale Caesar Salad with Olive Oil Breadcrumbs (page 25), Olive Oil Smashed Potatoes with Parmesan (page 135) and thin slices of Rich and Simple Dark Chocolate Cake (page 152).

STIR-FRIED PORK AND RICE NOODLE BOWL

3 tbsp (45 ml) Asian chili-garlic sauce

2 tbsp (30 ml) soy or tamari sauce

2 tbsp (30 ml) toasted sesame oil

1 tbsp (15 g) light brown sugar

¼ cup (60 ml) water

8 oz (227 g) dried rice pad Thai noodles

1 tbsp (15 ml) neutral oil, such as avocado or canola

1 cup (140 g) chopped red or yellow onion

1¼ lbs (570 g) ground pork

3 cloves garlic, grated on a microplane or finely chopped

1 tbsp (15 g) grated fresh ginger

1 fresh red chile pepper, chopped (or ½ tsp cayenne pepper)

3 green onions, white and light green parts sliced thin

Handful of fresh basil or cilantro

On those nights when you have a serious craving for takeout, make this salty, spicy, garlicky pork stir-fry instead. It's ready in 15 minutes or less and is one of those flavor-packed meals you'll be adding to your regular rotation. Serve over fragrant jasmine rice in place of rice noodles, or with cooked vegetables, such as bok choy or broccoli, for a lower-carb meal.

SERVES 4

Whisk together the chili sauce, soy sauce, sesame oil, brown sugar and water in a small bowl.

Cook the rice noodles in a large pot of boiling salted water, according to the package directions. Drain and rinse the noodles under cold running water so they don't stick together.

Heat the oil in a large nonstick skillet over medium-high heat. Add the onion and cook, stirring, until it's softened, about 3 minutes. Add the pork to the pan, and use a wooden spoon to break up the meat. Cook for about 5 minutes, until the meat is no longer pink, stirring frequently.

Stir in the garlic, ginger and chile pepper, and cook for 1 minute. Add the sauce. Cook a few minutes more, until the meat is coated in the sauce.

Remove the pan from the heat and stir in the noodles, tossing with a pair of tongs to coat the noodles in the sauce. Sprinkle the green onions and basil over the stir-fry and serve.

NOTE: Chili-garlic sauce is one of those magic little condiments that brings a meal together—kind of like harissa. My favorite brand is Lee Kum Kee.

THE BEST STEAK IS A SKIRT STEAK

2 lbs (910 g) skirt steak

2 tbsp (30 ml) fresh lemon juice

2 tbsp (30 ml) soy sauce or shoyu

2 tsp (10 g) finely chopped or grated garlic

1 tsp crushed red pepper

Flaky sea salt, such as Maldon

FOR A FAMILY-STYLE FEAST

Satisfy the omnivores at the table and serve the steak surrounded by vegetables. Pair the steak with Sweet Potato Wedges with Miso Butter (page 140), Spiced Roasted Carrots with Pistachios and Labneh (page 143) and Black Lentil Salad with Spinach and Goat Cheese (page 30). Make the Green Sauce on page 52 to serve on the side.

We eat steak only occasionally in our house, and when we do, I want it to be amazing. I'm talking about meat that's almost charred on the outside, juicy on the inside, with a ton of rich, beefy flavor. I look for a cut that isn't super fatty, one that has texture but isn't going to break the bank—which my second-favorite steak, the rib eye, can do. And I've found that skirt steak is the best steak for the money. It's a relatively lean cut from the rib plate section of the cow, an evenly flat piece of meat that isn't as tricky to cook as other cuts, which makes it friendly for home cooks. Sear the steak on top of the stove in a cast-iron skillet or use a really hot grill if you have one. The seasonings work their magic in a matter of minutes, but if you want to marinate the steak ahead of time, you can refrigerate it for up to one day before cooking.

SERVES 4–6

Put the steak on a plate or small rimmed baking sheet.

Combine the lemon juice, soy sauce, garlic and crushed red pepper in a small bowl and pour it over the meat. Let the steak sit at room temperature for 15 to 30 minutes, or cover and refrigerate it for up to 24 hours.

Heat a grill to medium-high indirect heat or place a lightly oiled large cast-iron skillet over high heat until it's very hot. Don't forget to turn on your exhaust fan if you're cooking indoors.

If you're cooking the steak on the stove, slice it into thirds and cook it in batches (if you have more than one pan, this is easier). Pat the steak with a paper towel to remove excess marinade.

Put the steak on the grill grate or in the hot pan and leave it there for 2 to 3 minutes, until it's turning crisp and brown on the edges. Flip the steak and cook the second side an additional 2 to 3 minutes for rare, or until it's cooked to your preference (although it's best not to cook it past medium-rare).

Let the steak rest on a cutting board for 10 minutes. Slice the steak into thin slices against the grain and sprinkle them lightly with the salt.

GOCHUJANG STEAK AND SCALLION SALAD

2 tbsp (60 g) gochujang paste

2 tbsp (36 g) white or red miso

1 tbsp (15 ml) honey

1 tbsp (15 ml) toasted sesame oil

2 tsp (10 g) grated fresh ginger

2 tsp (10 g) finely chopped or grated garlic

2 tbsp (30 ml) fresh lime juice

1 lb (455 g) beef top sirloin or boneless rib-eye steak, 1¼ inches (3 cm) thick

1 tsp kosher salt

Boston or bibb lettuce leaves

3 green onions, white and light green parts sliced thin

Fresh lime wedges

Ever since I first tasted gochujang, a Korean chili paste, I've been looking for ways to incorporate it into my cooking. I'm crazy about the way it tastes: slightly funky, savory and sweet all at once. This steak salad is an easy way to enjoy it—the rich earthy flavor of beef goes hand in hand with a gochujang marinade enriched by miso. The marinade does double duty as a dressing, adding a sweet-sour-salty flavor that's impossible to resist.

SERVES 4

Prepare a medium-hot grill for direct cooking.

Whisk together the gochujang, miso, honey, oil, ginger, garlic and lime juice in a bowl.

Sprinkle the steak on both sides with the salt. Pour 2 tablespoons (30 ml) of the gochujang mixture over the steak and turn it to coat it.

Grill the steak until it's well browned, about 6 minutes per side for medium-rare, or until done to your liking. Transfer the steak to a cutting board and let it rest for 10 minutes.

When you're ready to serve, cut the steak against the grain into thin slices. Arrange the lettuce on a large platter and drape the slices on top. Sprinkle the steak with the green onions. Squeeze the lime wedges over the salad and serve it with additional gochujang sauce on the side.

FOR A FAMILY-STYLE FEAST

The steak salad is fantastic alongside Chili-Garlic Cucumber Salad with Sesame (page 26), cooked short-grain rice and lots of cold beer.

MERGUEZ LAMB SLIDERS WITH GREEN SAUCE AND YOGURT TAHINI

GREEN SAUCE

1 tbsp (15 ml) white or red wine vinegar

½ tsp kosher salt

1 small green jalapeño or serrano chile pepper, thinly sliced

1 clove garlic, coarsely chopped

1½ cups (18 g) fresh cilantro leaves, coarsely chopped

1½ cups (12 g) fresh Italian parsley leaves, coarsely chopped

½ cup (120 ml) extra virgin olive oil

Fresh lemon juice, optional

SLIDERS

1 lb (455 g) ground lamb

1¼ tsp (4 g) kosher salt

1 tsp ground cumin

1 tsp ground coriander

1 tsp paprika

½ tsp freshly ground black pepper

½ tsp cayenne pepper

1 green onion, white and light green parts sliced thin

Yogurt-Tahini Sauce (page 73)

6 small burger buns or brioche buns, toasted

Sliced Persian cucumber

½ cup (60 g) crumbled feta cheese

About ½ cup (7 g) micro sprouts or fresh herb leaves

Lamb makes for out-of-this-world-delicious burgers, and I'd like everyone to know it. The ground meat's mildly earthy nature pairs exceptionally well with spices, which might explain why merguez, a classic Moroccan sausage, is so darn tasty. A slathering of two of my favorite pantry sauces—one a zesty, addictive green purée, the other a tangy yogurt blend—elevates these patties to next-level flavor. It's important not to cook beyond medium to keep them juicy.

MAKES 6 SLIDERS

To make the green sauce, put the vinegar in a small food processor and add the salt, jalapeño and garlic. Pile the cilantro and parsley on top, then pour in the oil. Pulse until the herbs are finely chopped and the sauce comes together to the consistency you prefer—with slight texture or creamy-smooth. Taste the sauce and season with additional salt and/or lemon juice, if you like.

To make the sliders, combine the lamb, salt, cumin, coriander, paprika, black pepper, cayenne and green onion in a bowl until the mixture is combined well. Form into six small patties to fit your burger buns. Prepare a medium-hot grill for direct cooking. Grill the patties until cooked to your preference, 2 to 3 minutes per side for medium-rare.

To assemble each slider, spread a layer of yogurt-tahini sauce on the top and bottom buns. Onto the bottom bun, stack a patty, some green sauce, a few slices of cucumber, some feta cheese, sprouts and finally the top bun.

NOTES: American lamb is a game changer for those accustomed to the overly gamy, muttony meat more commonly imported from Australia and New Zealand. I strongly urge you to seek it out and try it.

Green Sauce also goes with Super Creamy Homemade Hummus (page 17), Perfect Slow-Roasted Salmon (page 62) and The Best Steak is a Skirt Steak (page 48).

FOR A FAMILY-STYLE FEAST

Put the patties on a platter and serve them with the accompaniments on separate plates and bowls so each person can build their own burger.

HERBY SPATCHCOCK CHICKEN

3 tbsp (45 ml) extra virgin olive oil

1 tbsp (3 g) chopped fresh Italian parsley

1 tbsp (3 g) chopped fresh thyme

1 tbsp (3 g) chopped fresh sage

1 tbsp (14 g) finely chopped or grated garlic

1 tbsp (10 g) grated fresh lemon zest

½ tsp crushed red pepper

1½ tsp (5 g) kosher salt, plus more for seasoning the chicken

1 (3–4-lb [1.4–1.8-kg]) chicken

Spatchcock. You have to admit it sounds like a medieval word. But this recipe isn't from the Middle Ages. It actually describes the way a bird is opened up—or butterflied—by removing its backbone. This is a great way to roast a chicken because it cooks more evenly than if it were whole, with the breast and leg and thigh portions resting on the pan at the same level. Another plus: Once the chicken is flat, you have better access to the skin pockets, which is an open invite to apply tasty seasonings directly to the meat. I love to rub this fragrant herb paste under the skin to flavor the daylights out of it.

SERVES 4–6

Preheat the oven to 450°F (230°C), and oil a rimmed baking sheet.

Combine the olive oil, parsley, thyme, sage, garlic, zest, crushed red pepper and the 1½ teaspoons (5 g) of salt in a small bowl.

Put the chicken on a cutting board, breast side down. Cut along the backbone on either side with a pair of scissors and remove it.

Using your fingers, carefully separate the skin from the breast and thigh, being careful not to tear the skin. Smear the herb mixture under the skin onto the breast and thigh meat. Season the chicken generously with salt on both sides.

Put the chicken skin side down on the prepared baking sheet. Place a heavy skillet on top of the chicken to weigh it down—a cast-iron one is perfect.

Roast the chicken for 25 minutes, or until the skin is a rich brown, then remove the skillet and flip the chicken over. Use a spatula or a pair of tongs to do this, so you don't tear into the skin.

Continue roasting the chicken for an additional 20 to 25 minutes, until the juices run clear and the legs wiggle freely. The internal temperature should be 165°F (74°C).

Carve the chicken into pieces to serve.

FOR A FAMILY-STYLE FEAST

A showstopping meal matches this roasted chicken with Creamy Braised Leeks (page 144), Roasted Winter Squash and Shallots (page 139) and Olive Oil Smashed Potatoes with Parmesan (page 135).

BAKED HARISSA CHICKEN THIGHS WITH CHICKPEAS

2 plump shallots or ½ red onion, sliced into ½-inch (12-mm) wedges

1 (15-oz [425-g]) can chickpeas, drained

2 lbs (910 g) boneless skinless chicken thighs

2½ tsp (9 g) kosher salt, divided

1 pint (300 g) cherry tomatoes

2 tbsp (28 g) harissa paste (I like Les Moulins Mahjoub)

2 tbsp (30 ml) fresh lemon juice

2 tbsp (30 ml) extra virgin olive oil

2 cloves garlic, grated on a microplane or finely chopped

2 tsp (4 g) ground cumin

2 tsp (4 g) ground coriander

½ cup (6 g) fresh cilantro leaves

Harissa is a smoky, intensely savory chili paste with a gentle heat level and lots of earthy spice flavors—it's one of my all-time favorite condiments. Think of it as an ingredient that adds a magical layer of flavor. In this recipe, harissa plays a starring role as an element in both the sauce and the seasoning. This chicken supper is one of those meals that almost makes itself: Just mix everything in a baking dish, pop it into the oven and wait for seriously good aromas to waft through your kitchen.

SERVES 4–6

Preheat the oven to 450°F (230°C).

Spread the shallot slices and chickpeas evenly across the bottom of a 13 x 9 x 2-inch (33 x 23 x 5-cm) baking dish.

Season the chicken with 2 teaspoons (7 g) of the salt and arrange it on top of the shallot mixture. Distribute the tomatoes over the chicken, tucking them in here and there.

Stir together the harissa, lemon juice, olive oil, garlic, cumin, coriander and the remaining ½ teaspoon of salt in a small bowl. Spoon the harissa mixture evenly over the chicken and turn the pieces to coat both sides.

Bake for 25 to 30 minutes, until the chicken is cooked through and the tomatoes are burst and juicy.

Sprinkle the cilantro over the dish and serve it.

FOR A FAMILY-STYLE FEAST

Serve this with some cooked rice or couscous, because you don't want to miss the juicy pan sauce. Then serve slices of Orange Flower Olive Oil Cake (page 151) for dessert.

THAI BASIL CHICKEN

4 tbsp (60 ml) fish sauce, divided

2 tbsp (30 ml) sake or dry sherry

2 lbs (910 g) boneless, skinless chicken (breasts or thighs), sliced into 1½-inch (4-cm) chunks

2 tbsp (30 ml) tamari or soy sauce

1 tbsp (15 g) light brown sugar

1 tbsp (15 ml) chili-garlic sauce

1 tbsp (15 ml) water

2 tbsp (30 ml) roasted peanut oil or other high-heat vegetable oil

1 red bell pepper, sliced into ¼ inch (6-mm) strips

1 small red onion, thinly sliced

2–3 cloves garlic, thinly sliced

1 or 2 fresh red chile peppers, such as Thai or habanero (depending on your heat preference)

2 cups (24 g) fresh basil leaves

I can't tell you how many times my family has devoured this spicy, savory chicken. You'll find that it's a top-notch, one-dish-and-done meal you're going to want to make on repeat. And it's just as tasty if you substitute shrimp or ground pork in place of the chicken.

SERVES 4-6

Stir together 3 tablespoons (45 ml) of the fish sauce with the sake in a mixing bowl. Add the chicken to the bowl and toss to coat it with the mixture. Marinate the chicken for 15 minutes.

Mix the remaining tablespoon (15 ml) of fish sauce in a small bowl with the tamari, brown sugar, chili-garlic sauce and water until the sugar is dissolved. Set aside the mixture.

Heat a large (12 inch [31-cm]) cast-iron skillet or wok over medium-high heat until very hot. Add the oil and the marinated chicken to the pan and cook, stirring frequently, until the meat is seared and cooked through, 10 to 12 minutes.

Add the bell pepper and onion and continue cooking and stirring until the onion is softened, about 1 minute, then stir in the garlic and chile peppers.

Stir in the tamari mixture and bring it to a boil. Cook for another minute, then remove the pan from the heat and stir in the basil leaves.

FOR A FAMILY-STYLE FEAST

This saucy dish wants a sidekick, like cooked jasmine rice or rice noodles. The Chili-Garlic Cucumber Salad with Sesame (page 26) is a spot-on side.

SEAFOOD
TO SAVOR

EAT MORE FISH! If there's one thing you take away from this section, I very much hope it's a renewed (or just plain new) love for all of the delicious creatures that come out of the ocean.

My love for seafood might have to do with the fact that I grew up on the East Coast, as well as the family lore that some of my ancestors were fishermen, who ate their daily catch straight out of the Tyrrhenian Sea off the western coast of Italy—in which case it's genetic.

I narrowed down a very broad list in order to highlight seafoods that are relatively easy to find in markets and that take well to simple preparations. These include salmon and cod, shellfish (clams) and crustaceans (shrimp). And cephalopods, the taxonomic class that contains one of my favorite sea creatures, the squid, which I've featured in a dish I crave regularly: Salt-and-Pepper Calamari with Cherry Tomatoes (page 77).

Yes, good-quality seafood can be expensive. Fish is becoming more and more scarce and, as a result, it is that much more of a treasure. Especially wild fish. It's kind of crazy when you realize that seafood is one of the last true wild foods we eat regularly in the modern world.

I opt for salmon as often as possible (although wild salmon can be breathtakingly pricey), as well as cod and other easy-to-cook flaky white fish. Clams and squid are economically priced and abundant, making them a great choice in terms of sustainability.

The recipes in this chapter highlight some of my favorite ways to cook seafood—you'll find my take on the classic Italian-style combo of clams, pasta and white wine sauce (page 67) and a one-skillet Mediterranean cod with spicy tomato sauce and white beans (page 65).

PERFECT
SLOW-ROASTED SALMON

1 bunch fresh tender herbs, such as Italian parsley, basil, dill or cilantro, stems trimmed off

1 (2-lb [910-g]) center-cut king salmon fillet, with skin on

2 tsp (7 g) kosher salt

1 tbsp (15 ml) extra virgin olive oil

2 tsp (7 g) grated fresh lime or orange zest

½ tsp paprika

¼ tsp ground turmeric

One summer night a few years back, I preheated my outdoor gas grill as low as it would go. I wanted to try a method, from Samin Nosrat's book *Salt Fat Acid Heat*, for gently roasting a beautiful Alaskan king salmon. I had been very fortunate to purchase the salmon from a top fish purveyor in New York City, so it was incredibly fresh, and I knew it would taste delicious. But I didn't know that slow-roasting it would be a game changer. That fish turned out so meltingly tender and flavorful—with only minimal seasoning—it almost brought tears to my eyes. Since then, I've been preparing salmon and other varieties of fatty fish this way—using my grill or oven—whenever I get the chance. I encourage you to make this recipe whenever you get your hands on the choicest king salmon, halibut or other suitably fatty fish.

SERVES 4-6

Preheat the oven to 300°F (150°C).

Arrange the herbs over the bottom of a rectangular baking dish. Lay the salmon fillet, skin side down, on top of the herbs. Season the salmon generously with the salt and drizzle it with the oil.

Sprinkle the zest, paprika and turmeric over the fish and rub so they are evenly dispersed over the flesh.

Bake the salmon for 25 to 35 minutes, depending on the thickness of your fish. When it's ready, the thickest part of the fish will feel firm to the touch, and it will flake when gently prodded with a dull knife. If you like, test that the interior temperature reads 120°F (50°C) on an instant-read thermometer

Run a spatula between the skin and the fish to separate them, and serve the fish broken into rustic, imperfect pieces.

FOR A FAMILY-STYLE FEAST

A beautiful piece of fish deserves to be the center of attention, but just like any celebrity, it's even better with an entourage. Pass around Falafel-Spiced Chickpea Salad (page 33) and Spiced Roasted Carrots with Pistachios and Labneh (page 143) to go with the salmon.

PORTUGUESE COD WITH PEPPERONI AND WHITE BEANS

COD

1½ lbs (680 g) wild cod fillet, cut into 6-oz (170-g) pieces

Kosher salt

Black pepper from a pepper grinder

3 tbsp (45 ml) extra virgin olive oil

3 tbsp (23 g) sliced shallot

2 cloves garlic, sliced

2 oz (55 g) pepperoni or spicy salami, sliced into ¼-inch (6-mm)-thick half-moons

½ tsp smoked paprika

¼ tsp cayenne pepper

½ cup (120 ml) dry white wine

1 (14-oz [400-g]) can cherry tomatoes or diced tomatoes, drained

1 cup (60 g) cooked or canned cannellini beans, drained

1 tsp chopped fresh thyme

I'm one-quarter Portuguese on my mother's side, but for some reason I didn't grow up eating much Portuguese food. I remember my grandmother cooked a traditional soup with linguiça, potatoes and cabbage, but for the most part I've had to discover the cuisine of this beautiful country on my own. Situated on the Iberian Peninsula, Portugal's entire coastline fronts the North Atlantic Ocean, which makes it a mecca for fresh seafood. This recipe was inspired by a simple Portuguese-style fishermen's stew, with smoky spice, creamy white beans and bits of pepperoni to add depth of flavor and a hint of heat. As a finishing touch, almond breadcrumbs provide textural crunch. You can make this dinner in less than 30 minutes.

SERVES 4-6

For the cod, on a plate, generously sprinkle the fish with salt on both sides and season it with about six grinds of coarse black pepper.

Place a large (12-inch [31-cm]) skillet over medium high heat and let it heat until a drop of water sizzles on contact. Add the olive oil, shallot, garlic, pepperoni, paprika and cayenne. Cook until the pepperoni starts to take on some color, 3 to 4 minutes, stirring frequently. Keep your eye on the heat level to make sure the garlic doesn't turn brown too quickly.

Pour in the wine. Let it bubble, then cook until it is reduced by half, about 3 minutes. Add the tomatoes, beans, thyme and ½ teaspoon of salt. Simmer the sauce, uncovered, for 10 minutes to thicken it slightly.

Nestle the cod in the sauce. Cover the pan and lower the heat to a simmer. Cook for 10 to 14 minutes, until the cod looks opaque and the fish easily breaks into large white flakes.

(continued)

ALMOND BREADCRUMBS

¼ cup (30 g) Marcona or whole roasted unsalted almonds

2 tbsp (8 g) coarse fresh breadcrumbs

2 tbsp (6 g) chopped fresh Italian parsley

2 tbsp (30 ml) extra virgin olive oil

To make the topping, while the cod is simmering, pulse the almonds, breadcrumbs and parsley in a small food processor to make large, rustic crumbs. You can also just do this by hand—chop the almonds and parsley and stir them together with the breadcrumbs.

Place a small skillet over medium-high heat and add the olive oil. Spread the crumbs in the pan and stir to coat them with the oil. Cook until the mixture smells toasty, about 2 minutes.

Sprinkle ¼ cup (30 g) of the almond crumbs over the fish. Serve in shallow bowls, with additional crumbs on the side.

FOR A FAMILY-STYLE FEAST

This is one of the dishes to serve when you want to impress family and friends without breaking a sweat. Have a loaf of crusty bread ready to go, and eat the cod with Garlicky Greens with Olive Oil (page 128) and some Romesco Sauce (page 71).

WHITE WINE CLAMS WITH ARTICHOKES AND TOASTED ORZO

1½ cups (260 g) orzo

3 tbsp (45 ml) extra virgin olive oil, divided

1 fennel bulb, stems trimmed and bulb sliced thin

¼ cup (40 g) chopped shallots

3 cloves garlic, thinly sliced

½ tsp crushed red pepper

Kosher salt

½ cup (120 ml) dry white wine

36 littleneck clams, cleaned (see sidebar on page 68)

Here's a recipe based on the classic flavors of linguine and clam sauce. To switch things up a little, I like to serve the clams and their tangy, buttery, garlicky broth over plump marinated artichoke hearts and toasted orzo pasta. This dish is a perfect gateway to the joys of shellfish; if cooking or eating clams has been a deal-breaker for you, this recipe may well change your mind. Quickly steaming fresh clams in white wine is one of the simplest ways to enjoy them—they taste purely of the ocean and are absolutely delicious.

SERVES 4-6

Spread out the orzo in a dry medium skillet and place it over medium-high heat. Toast until it's golden-brown and nutty smelling, about 10 minutes. Toss the pan frequently so the orzo toasts evenly. Remove the pan from the heat.

Cook the orzo in 2 to 3 quarts (1.9 to 2.8 L) of boiling salted water until al dente, following the package directions. Drain the orzo, and transfer it to a bowl. Stir in 1 tablespoon (15 ml) of the olive oil and cover the bowl to keep the pasta warm.

Place a large pan with at least 3-inch (8-cm)-high sides over medium-high heat. Add the remaining 2 tablespoons (30 ml) of olive oil, fennel, shallots, garlic, crushed red pepper and a pinch of salt. Cook for 2 to 3 minutes, stirring occasionally, until the vegetables are softened and the garlic is aromatic.

Pour in the wine, and let it bubble for 30 seconds. Add the clams in one layer, and cover the pan. Cook for 5 minutes, then lift the lid and take a peek. Stir the clams around. If they're not all opened, replace the cover and continue cooking an additional 3 to 5 minutes, depending on the size of the clams.

(continued)

1½ cups (170 g) marinated artichoke hearts, drained and halved (from a 10–12-oz [280–340-g] jar)

¼ cup (10 g) chopped fresh Italian parsley

3 tbsp (45 g) unsalted butter

2 cups (40 g) baby arugula

2 tbsp (20 g) grated fresh lemon zest

Add the artichoke hearts, parsley and butter to the pan, and give everything a good stir.

To serve, portion the orzo into wide bowls. Add some arugula to each bowl and spoon some of the clams and broth over each serving. Sprinkle with the lemon zest. Set an empty bowl or two on the table for the clam shells.

HOW TO CLEAN CLAMS

Clams are a no-brainer to cook. They don't require slicing or dicing and they're ready to eat in minutes—literally! It's the task of cleaning them that requires a bit of special attention. The process is as easy as can be, and it's kind of an important step, because a mouthful of sand is not fun to eat.

First, sort through the clams and discard any whose shells are cracked or broken. Place the clams in a colander under cold running water, at the same time using your hands (or a small brush) to rub off any sand on the surface of the shells. Transfer the clams to a large bowl as you go.

Fill the bowl with cold water and swish the clams around vigorously. Let them sit for a few minutes, then lift them out of the water and transfer them to the colander to drain. Pour out the water in the bowl—there will likely be some sand on the bottom. Put the clams back in the bowl and add more fresh water. Repeat the soaking and draining until you don't see any sand or grit on the bottom of the bowl. If you notice a shell that remains open throughout the cleaning and swishing, the clam is probably dead. Throw it out.

NOTE: Many supermarkets sell clams that are farm raised; they won't be as sandy as wild ones.

OREGANO SHRIMP WITH FETA AND ROMESCO SAUCE

ROMESCO SAUCE

2 red bell peppers

¼ cup (30 g) whole roasted unsalted almonds

1 clove garlic, chopped

2 tbsp (30 ml) sherry or red wine vinegar

½ tsp kosher salt

¼ tsp cayenne pepper

¼ cup (60 ml) extra virgin olive oil

SHRIMP

1 lb (455 g) shrimp, peeled and deveined (I use 16–20 size)

1 clove garlic, grated on a microplane or finely chopped

1 tsp crushed red pepper

1 tsp smoked paprika

2 tbsp (6 g) chopped fresh oregano or 2 tsp (2 g) dried

2 tbsp (30 ml) extra virgin olive oil, divided

1 tsp kosher salt

1 pint (300 g) cherry tomatoes, halved

½ cup (120 ml) chicken or vegetable broth or water

½ cup (60 g) crumbled feta cheese

When I talk about making dinner on the fly, I often use this meal as an example. It's a tasty, ever-so-slightly Greek-inspired dish that's sauced with roasted red pepper romesco—which is one of my essential pantry sauces. Make the sauce first and the whole thing comes together in minutes. Keep frozen shrimp on hand, and they'll become your best friend when you want something quick. Pull them out of the freezer 15 minutes before you want to cook, and pile them in a bowl in the sink under cold running water until they're thawed.

SERVES 4–6

To make the sauce, roast the peppers directly on a hot grill or under a broiler until they are blackened on all sides, about 10 to 15 minutes. Transfer the peppers to a bowl and, when they are cool enough to handle, remove and discard the skin, seeds and stems.

Place the peppers in a mini food processor or a blender, and add the almonds, garlic, sherry, salt, cayenne and oil. Process until the sauce is very smooth, about 1 minute. Taste and add more salt or sherry, if needed. You can keep the sauce in the refrigerator for up to 5 days; bring it to room temperature before serving.

To prepare the shrimp, toss them in a large bowl with the garlic, crushed red pepper, paprika, oregano, 1 tablespoon (15 ml) of the olive oil and the salt.

Heat the remaining 1 tablespoon (15 ml) of olive oil in a large skillet over medium-high heat. Add the cherry tomatoes and sauté them until the tomatoes begin to blister and release their juices, about 3 minutes.

(continued)

FOR A FAMILY-STYLE FEAST

Put a bowl of Rosemary and Fennel Roasted Almonds (page 14) on the table and serve the shrimp with cooked pearl couscous, quinoa or another grain and Broccoli Rabe with Chili and Pecorino (page 132).

Add the shrimp to the pan. Cook the shrimp for about 2 minutes, flipping them over once they begin to turn pink on the bottom. Continue cooking until they are cooked through, about 5 minutes total.

Stir in ¼ cup (60 ml) of the romesco sauce along with the broth, and simmer for a few minutes to thicken the sauce.

Remove the pan from the heat. Sprinkle the feta over the shrimp and serve it with additional sauce on the side.

BRANZINO
WITH FRIED LEMONS

YOGURT-TAHINI SAUCE

⅓ cup (80 g) thick plain yogurt, such as Greek- or Icelandic-style

¼ cup (55 g) tahini

2 tbsp (30 ml) extra virgin olive oil

2 tbsp (30 ml) fresh lemon juice

1 tbsp (15 ml) cold water

1 tsp za'atar

½ tsp finely chopped or grated garlic

½ tsp kosher salt

¼ tsp cayenne pepper

BRANZINO

6 skin-on branzino fillets (about 1½ lbs [680 g])

2 tsp (7 g) grated fresh lemon zest

2 tsp (2 g) chopped fresh thyme

Kosher salt and freshly ground black pepper

2 slices crusty sourdough bread, cut into cubes

3 tbsp (45 ml) extra virgin olive oil, divided

2 small lemons, halved

2 tbsp (6 g) chopped fresh Italian parsley

Flaky sea salt, such as Maldon

Branzino (called *loup de mer* in French) is a type of Mediterranean sea bass that has a mild, nutty-sweet taste that even self-declared fish haters will go for. It matches up perfectly with zingy, bold seasonings like lemon and garlic. And the crunchy breadcrumbs sprinkled over the cooked fish provide a welcome contrast to the fish's delicate texture. I love to serve this dish with a creamy yogurt-tahini sauce for added richness. Branzino is often sold whole—ask your fishmonger to fillet it for you.

SERVES 4-6

For the sauce, whisk the yogurt, tahini, oil, lemon juice, water, za'atar, garlic, salt and cayenne in a bowl, or pulse it in a mini food processor, until the mixture is smooth and creamy. If necessary, add more water, drop by drop. You're looking for a thick, spreadable consistency. Taste and add more salt, lemon juice or pepper, if needed, to suit your taste. You can refrigerate the sauce for 3 to 5 days, if you'd like to make it ahead (it will thicken a bit).

To make the branzino, preheat the oven to 400°F (200°C).

Put the branzino fillets on a work surface. Pat the skin side dry with paper towels. Sprinkle the flesh side of the fish evenly with the lemon zest, thyme, salt and pepper, rubbing in the seasonings lightly. Set the fish aside for 10 to 15 minutes.

Pulse the bread cubes in a small food processor or blender until they form coarse crumbs. Heat 1 tablespoon (15 ml) of the olive oil in a large, ovenproof skillet over medium-high heat. Add the crumbs and stir them to coat them in the oil. Cook until the crumbs turn golden brown and smell toasty, about 5 minutes. Scrape the crumbs into a small bowl.

Pour 1 tablespoon (15 ml) of the remaining olive oil in each of two large, ovenproof skillets, and place them over medium-high heat until the oil starts to shimmer. Put one halved lemon in each pan, flesh side down. Sear the lemons until they're golden brown, about 2 minutes. Move the lemons to the side of the pan and add three fish fillets, skin side down, to each pan, pressing on the fillets with a spatula.

(continued)

BRANZINO
WITH FRIED LEMONS (CONT.)

FOR A FAMILY-STYLE FEAST

This makes a perfect light and elegant meal. The lemony flavors in this dish go with Italian White Beans and Greens (page 136) and Roasted Za'atar Cauliflower Salad (page 22).

Cook the fish until the skin starts to brown and crisp, about 3 minutes. Transfer the pans to the oven, and bake until the fish is opaque and cooked through, about 5 minutes.

To serve, spread the yogurt-tahini sauce over the bottom of a large platter. Arrange the fish on top of the sauce and squeeze the juice from the fried lemons over the fish. Sprinkle ⅓ cup (22 g) of the breadcrumbs and the parsley over the fish. The remaining breadcrumbs will keep for 5 days in a covered container. Crush a large pinch of the sea salt between your fingers and scatter it over the fish.

SALT-AND-PEPPER CALAMARI
WITH CHERRY TOMATOES

1 lb (455 g) cleaned squid bodies and tentacles

¼ cup (60 ml) extra virgin olive oil, plus more for serving

3 cloves garlic, grated on a microplane or finely chopped

¼ cup (10 g) chopped fresh Italian parsley

1 tsp dried oregano

1 tsp crushed red pepper

¾ tsp kosher salt

½ tsp freshly ground black pepper

1 pint (300 g) cherry tomatoes, halved

12 oz (340 g) hot cooked linguine or spaghetti

4 lemon wedges

Pinch of flaky sea salt, such as Maldon

Let's agree right now that calamari—aka squid—does not get enough love in the world of everyday cooking. But it should! It's inexpensive, it's packed with lean protein and it cooks in about 5 minutes. More important, because it has a mild flavor, squid is the perfect blank canvas for all the spicy, lemony, garlicky flavors going on in this dish. Before you rule squid out of your meal planning, please try this.

SERVES 4-6

Slice the squid bodies into ½-inch (12-mm)-wide rings. Pat the squid bodies and tentacles dry with a towel. Toss the squid in a large bowl with the olive oil, garlic, parsley, oregano, crushed red pepper, salt and black pepper.

Heat a large (12-inch [31-cm]) skillet over high heat for 3 to 5 minutes, until a drop of water instantly sizzles and evaporates.

Dump the squid into the pan in one layer. Cook, shaking the pan frequently, until the squid turn white and opaque, which should take less than 5 minutes. If your pan is smaller than 12 inches (31 cm), cook the squid in two batches. Stir in the tomatoes and cook for another minute or two to warm them up.

Put the pasta in a large serving bowl, and pour the squid and all the juices from the pan over it. Squeeze the lemon wedges over everything, and generously drizzle the squid and tomatoes with olive oil. Sprinkle the dish with the flaky salt and serve.

NOTE: Most of the time, the squid you'll find in the fish case at the market has already been cleaned, previously frozen and thawed. You can also buy blocks of frozen squid and defrost them yourself—place the unpackaged squid in a large bowl of cold water until it's pliable, changing the water a few times. Drain the squid well and pat very dry before using it.

SLOW-
COOKED
SUPPERS

WHEN IT COMES TO FAMILY FAVORITES IN MY HOUSE, slow-cooked dishes always rank near the top, right up there with pasta.

It's no wonder they bring so much pleasure. My deeply savory beef stew topped with fluffy Gruyère cheese dumplings (page 80) is the essence of cozy comfort food—my son begs me to make it all year round.

The (mostly) hands-off simplicity of slow cooking is appealing in itself: Put everything in a pot, walk away and get on with your day while the house fills with delicious smells. When it's serving time, put the whole pot right on the table and have everyone help themselves.

And then there are the leftovers. They're what family cooking is all about: food that tastes even better the next day (and sometimes the day after that), always on hand to share with surprise guests or reheat for supper on a quiet night in.

I reach all around the global flavor box with these recipes: Sunday Sauce Pork Ragu (page 91), Coconut-Lime Chicken Curry (page 83) and Beer-Braised Pulled Pork (page 87), the last of which is saturated in Mexican flavors that make it a must for piling onto fresh tortillas on build-your-own-taco nights.

BEEF STEW WITH HERBED GRUYÈRE DUMPLINGS

STEW

3½ lbs (1.6 kg) boneless beef chuck roast, trimmed of fat and cut into 2–3-inch (5–8-cm) cubes

1 tbsp plus 2 tsp (17 g) kosher salt, divided

1–4 tbsp (15–60 ml) extra virgin olive oil, divided

¾ cup (180 ml) dry red wine

1 yellow onion, chopped

10 oz (280 g) carrots (about 4 medium), cut into 2-inch (5-cm) pieces

2 leeks, white parts halved lengthwise and chopped

¼ cup (40 g) whole cloves garlic, halved

3 tbsp (45 g) tomato paste

2 tsp (3 g) herbes de Provence or chopped fresh thyme

There's something magnificent about bringing a jumbo pot of hearty beef stew to the table, especially when it's chock-full of fall-apart-tender chunks of meat and vegetables. And the soft, herby, cheesy dumplings that cook right in the pot are literally the topping on the cake. Making stew does require work up front—plan on a good 30 minutes of prep. But the payoff is huge. Once everything is in the pot, you walk away while the stew simmers, filling your home with a mouthwatering aroma. And, as we all know, stew is even better the next day.

SERVES 4-6

For the stew, cut a piece of parchment paper the size of the cover of a large (6- to 7-quart [5.7- to 6.6-L]) Dutch oven or large, heavy-bottomed pot.

Season the beef cubes evenly with 1 tablespoon (10 g) of the salt.

Put the Dutch oven over medium-high heat and let it get hot for a few minutes; a splash of water should sizzle and evaporate on contact.

Add 1 tablespoon (15 ml) of the oil. Arrange some of the beef in one layer in the pot, without crowding the pieces. Cook until the meat is nicely brown, about 3 minutes per side. Transfer the beef to a large bowl.

Repeat with the remaining beef in one or two more batches, adding a bit more oil each time, as needed, to coat the bottom of the pan.

Pour in the wine and let it bubble for a few seconds. Use a wooden spoon to scrape up all the brown bits from the bottom of the pot. Cook the wine until it's reduced by about half, about 3 to 4 minutes, then pour it over the meat in the bowl.

Add 2 tablespoons (30 ml) of the olive oil to the pot and stir in the onion, carrots, leeks and garlic. Cook for 5 minutes, or until the onion is softened. Add the tomato paste and herbes de Provence, and stir them into the vegetables.

(continued)

1 lb (455 g) Yukon Gold potatoes, cut into 1½-inch (4-cm) chunks

¼ cup (35 g) all-purpose flour

1 bay leaf

Freshly ground black pepper

4 cups (960 ml) beef or chicken broth

DUMPLINGS

1 cup (140 g) all-purpose flour

1 tsp baking powder

1 tsp kosher salt

½ tsp baking soda

½ tsp granulated sugar

¾ cup (180 ml) buttermilk

¼ cup (60 ml) melted butter

2 oz (55 g) grated Gruyère cheese

1 tbsp (3 g) chopped fresh Italian parsley

1 tbsp (2 g) chopped fresh tarragon or chives

FOR SERVING

Grated Gruyère cheese

¼ cup (8 g) coarsely chopped fresh Italian parsley

Add the reserved beef, potatoes, flour, bay leaf and remaining 2 teaspoons (7 g) of salt to the pot. Season generously with the pepper, and stir to mix everything together. Pour in the broth and bring it to a simmer. Press the prepared parchment paper lightly over the stew, then cover it with the pot lid.

Cook at a gentle simmer for 2 hours—keep your eye on the heat and adjust as necessary so the stew doesn't come to a full boil.

Remove the lid and parchment paper, and continue cooking the stew for 15 minutes (you may need to raise the heat to reach a simmer).

Make the dumplings while the stew simmers. In a medium bowl, stir together the flour, baking powder, salt, baking soda, sugar, buttermilk, butter, cheese, parsley and tarragon, just until the dough comes together. When the stew has simmered uncovered for 15 minutes, scoop generous ¼-cup (55-g) portions of the dough and place them on top of the simmering stew. Cook the dumplings uncovered for 5 minutes. Cover the pot and cook for 15 minutes, until the dumplings are puffed and cooked through.

Serve the stew in bowls (be sure to remove the bay leaf), topped with the dumplings and sprinkled with the additional cheese and parsley.

COCONUT-LIME CHICKEN CURRY

1 tbsp (15 ml) avocado or canola oil

⅓ cup (50 g) chopped shallot

2 fresh red chile peppers or jalapeños, chopped

1½ cups (225 g) chopped carrots (2-inch [5-cm] pieces)

1 red bell pepper, seeded and chopped into 2-inch (5-cm) pieces

2-inch (5-cm) knob ginger, peeled and finely chopped

2 cloves garlic, grated on a microplane or finely chopped

3 tbsp (45 ml) Thai red curry paste

3 tbsp (45 ml) fish sauce

1½ tbsp (18 g) coconut sugar or light brown sugar

¾ cup (180 ml) chicken broth, for Dutch-oven preparation; ½ cup (120 ml) for pressure or slow cooker

2½ lbs (1.2 kg) boneless, skinless chicken thighs, cut into 2-inch (5-cm) chunks

1 cup (240 ml) canned coconut milk (not light), stirred well to incorporate the creamy top with the watery liquid on the bottom

3 cups (60 g) baby spinach leaves

3 green onions, white and light green parts sliced on a diagonal

¼ cup (3 g) fresh cilantro leaves

2 tbsp (30 ml) fresh lime juice

Cooked rice noodles or jasmine rice

Fresh lime wedges

Make this intensely flavorful chicken fit into your life any way you can. You have choices: Make it in your electric pressure cooker, in your slow cooker or on the stovetop. The brothy sauce is tangy, creamy and sweet with coconut—a perfect match for rice noodles or jasmine rice.

SERVES 4-6

SLOW COOKER

Coat the bottom of a medium skillet with the oil. Sauté the shallot, chile peppers, carrots and bell pepper for about 3 to 5 minutes, until they soften, stirring occasionally. Stir in the ginger, garlic and curry paste and cook for 1 minute.

Transfer the mixture to a slow cooker pot and add the fish sauce, sugar, broth and chicken.

Cook on the high setting for 2 hours or on low for 4 hours.

Add the coconut milk and cook uncovered until the liquid reduces, 25 to 30 minutes. Stir in the spinach, green onions, cilantro and lime juice and serve over the noodles, topped with the lime wedges.

STOVETOP

Heat the oil in a large pot or Dutch oven over medium heat. Add the shallot, chile peppers, carrots and bell pepper and cook until the vegetables are softened, stirring occasionally, for 3 to 5 minutes. Stir in the ginger, garlic and curry paste.

Add the fish sauce, sugar and broth, and cook for 1 minute.

Put the chicken in the pot and bring the mixture to a simmer, then lower the heat and cook the curry for 25 minutes, partially covered, until the chicken is very tender.

Stir in the coconut milk, spinach, green onions, cilantro and lime juice. Serve in bowls over the noodles or rice, topped with the lime wedges.

(continued)

PRESSURE COOKER

Set the sauté function on your pressure cooker to high. Add the oil, shallot, chile peppers, carrots and bell pepper, and cook until they soften, stirring occasionally. Stir in the ginger, garlic and curry paste and cook for 1 minute.

Add the fish sauce, sugar, broth and chicken to the pressure cooker pot. Lock the lid in place and cook on high pressure for 6 minutes. Release the pressure manually.

Stir in the coconut milk, spinach, green onions, cilantro and lime juice and serve in bowls over the noodles, topped with the lime wedges.

BEER-BRAISED
PULLED PORK

3–4 lbs (1.4–1.8 kg) boneless pork shoulder, cut into 3 or 4 large pieces

1 tbsp plus 2 tsp (17 g) kosher salt

1 tbsp (15 ml) avocado or canola oil

1 (12-oz [360 ml]) can lager style beer

1 large white or yellow onion, peeled and cut into wedges

6 cloves garlic, smashed with a large knife

2 jalapeño peppers, halved

1 tbsp (6 g) ground cumin

1 tbsp (6 g) paprika

2 dried chiles de arbol or dried chipotles

1 bay leaf

FOR A FAMILY-STYLE FEAST

Put some crumbled queso fresco, sliced avocado, fresh lime wedges and hot sauce on the table alongside the pork, served in a big bowl, so people can choose their own adventure. Or, add the shredded meat to Black Bean Tostadas with Avocado Mash (page 18).

This is as good as it gets: tangy, melt-in-your-mouth pork loaded up with spices and aromatics. I have to warn you that the smell that floats through the house while this cooks will quite possibly drive you crazy with hunger. When the pork is done, you have options for serving: Make a pulled-pork sandwich, doused with your favorite barbecue sauce; assemble the tastiest tacos on corn tortillas, garnished just the way you like with salsa and your favorite fixings; or serve it over rice.

SERVES 4–6

Season the meat on all sides with the salt.

Place a large skillet over medium-high heat and let it get hot for a few minutes; a splash of water should sizzle and evaporate on contact.

Add the oil to the pan, then add the pork pieces. Sear the pork, in batches if necessary, until it is browned on all sides, about 5 minutes per side. Transfer the meat to an electric pressure cooker or slow cooker.

PRESSURE COOKER

Pour in the beer and add the onion, garlic, jalapeños, cumin, paprika, chiles and bay leaf. Secure the lid on the machine. Cook on high pressure for 45 minutes in an electric pressure cooker, allowing the pressure to release naturally.

Remove the pork from the cooking pot and place it in a large bowl. Shred the meat into pieces—two forks work perfectly for this. Skim excess fat from the cooking liquid, remove the bay leaf and pour enough of the skimmed liquid over the pork to moisten it.

SLOW COOKER

Pour in the beer and add the onion, garlic, jalapeños, cumin, paprika, chiles and bay leaf. Cook the pork for 4 hours on high or 6 hours on low, until the meat is very tender when prodded with a fork.

Remove the pork from the cooking pot and place it in a large bowl. Shred the meat into pieces—two forks work perfectly for this. Skim excess fat from the cooking liquid, remove the bay leaf and pour enough of the skimmed liquid over the pork to moisten it.

FALL-APART BEEF SHORT RIBS IN RED WINE

4 lbs (1.8 kg) bone-in beef short ribs, in 2-inch (5-cm)-wide pieces

2 tbsp (20 g) kosher salt

1½ cups (360 ml) full-bodied, dry red wine such as Côtes-du-Rhône, Malbec or Zinfandel, divided

1 cup (240 ml) beef or chicken broth or water

1 whole head garlic, halved

Handful of fresh thyme sprigs

Whenever I discover a new method for cooking something that cuts out multiple ingredients, saves a bunch of time and yet somehow makes it taste even better—I put it down as a keeper. That's what these lip-smacking, tender and meaty short ribs are. This is as basic a braise as you could ask for, one that requires only a handful of ingredients and two pans. The oven does all the magic here, first at high heat to sear the meat and then much lower to cook it very slowly. You end up with the essence of rich beefy flavor and meat that falls into delectable shreds at the touch of a fork.

SERVES 4–6

Preheat the oven to 475°F (240°C).

Arrange the short ribs on a large rimmed baking sheet. Sprinkle them generously on all sides with the salt.

Roast the ribs for 20 minutes, until the meat is sizzling and forming a brown crust on the pan. Transfer the ribs to a roasting pan or baking dish large enough to hold the ribs snugly in one layer.

Reduce the oven temperature to 275°F (135°C).

Pour ½ cup (120 ml) of the wine onto the sheet pan. Scrape up the brown bits with a spatula and pour them and the wine over the short ribs. Add the remaining 1 cup (240 ml) of wine and the broth. Tuck the garlic and thyme sprigs in and around the meat.

Cover the pan tightly with aluminum foil and return it to the oven. Bake for 3½ hours. The meat should be very tender, breaking apart into pieces when prodded with a fork. Remove the pan from the oven and let the meat rest, covered, for 20 minutes.

Skim the excess fat from the surface, if you like, and serve.

FOR A FAMILY-STYLE FEAST

Cozy dinner alert: Make the short ribs and serve them along with Olive Oil Smashed Potatoes with Parmesan (page 135) and Charred Broccoli Salad (page 29).

SUNDAY SAUCE PORK RAGU

3½–4 lbs (1.6–1.8 kg) boneless pork shoulder, trimmed of fat and cut into 2 or 3 chunks

Kosher salt

2 tbsp (30 ml) extra virgin olive oil

1 yellow onion, chopped

5 whole cloves garlic

2 carrots, finely chopped

1 tsp fennel seeds

½–1 tsp crushed red pepper

1 tbsp (3 g) chopped fresh rosemary

¾ cup (180 ml) dry red wine

2 tbsp (30 g) tomato paste

1 (28-oz [794-g]) can crushed tomatoes

2 cups (480 ml) chicken broth

¼ cup (12 g) finely chopped fresh Italian parsley

Cooked pasta or polenta

Freshly grated Pecorino Romano cheese

This is home-style food at its best: tender shreds of slow-cooked pork shoulder merged with a rich sauce made with tomato and red wine. Served with pasta or over polenta, it's the ultimate Sunday dinner. Leftovers are a bonus.

SERVES 4–6

Arrange a rack in the middle of the oven, and preheat it to 450°F (230°C). Cut a circle of parchment paper the size of the cover of a large Dutch oven.

Season the pork very generously with salt on all sides. Place the pork on a rimmed baking sheet and roast it for 20 minutes. Pour off the rendered fat, and refrigerate it for another use. Reduce the oven temperature to 325°F (165°C).

Meanwhile, heat the olive oil over medium heat in the Dutch oven. Add the onion, garlic and carrots and cook, stirring occasionally, until the onion is translucent and the carrots are softened. Stir in the fennel seeds, crushed red pepper and rosemary, and cook for 30 seconds. Pour in the red wine, and bring it to a boil. Let it bubble until it is reduced by half, about 10 minutes. Stir in the tomato paste, tomatoes, broth and 1½ teaspoons (7 g) of salt.

Nestle the pork chunks in the liquid. Place the prepared parchment paper over the pot, pressing it down so it touches the pork. Cover the pan with a lid and put it in the oven, on the middle rack. Cook for 3 hours—the meat should be very tender when prodded with a fork.

When the meat is done, remove it to a large bowl and shred it with two forks. Pour the liquid in the pot through a mesh strainer set over a large bowl, reserving the vegetable solids. Skim the fat off the strained liquid and return the liquid to the pot, along with the reserved vegetables, the shredded pork and the parsley.

Warm the sauce over low heat. Serve the ragu over pasta or polenta, and sprinkle it with the grated cheese.

FOR A FAMILY-STYLE FEAST

For a standout Sunday—actually, any day—dinner, serve the ragu with Broccoli Rabe with Chili and Pecorino (page 132) and a Big Green Salad (page 34).

PINOT GRIGIO–BRAISED CHICKEN THIGHS

6 bone-in, skin-on chicken thighs

Kosher salt

1 tbsp (10 g) brown rice flour or all-purpose flour

2 tbsp (30 ml) extra virgin olive oil

4 whole cloves garlic, halved

½ cup (120 ml) pinot grigio or other dry white wine

2 shallots, quartered lengthwise

½ cup (120 ml) chicken broth

1 tbsp (15 g) Dijon mustard

3 sprigs fresh thyme, plus 1 tsp fresh leaves for serving

Freshly ground black pepper

FOR A FAMILY-STYLE FEAST

Bring the trattoria home! Serve this braised chicken with Charred Broccoli Salad (page 29) and Roasted Winter Squash and Shallots (page 139), along with some bread to soak up the sauce.

Chicken thighs are your friend. They deliver the best bang for your chicken buck, hands down. This preparation yields fall-apart-tender chicken in a tangy wine sauce. The bonus in this dish is the garlic: The halved whole cloves turn so sweet and soft in the braise that they melt in your mouth like tender beans. Salting chicken overnight is a restaurant trick I learned on the job and it's a game changer. Not only does it help the skin to crisp, but it makes the chicken tasty through and through. If you're short on time, even 10 to 15 minutes will work.

SERVES 4–6

Pat the chicken thighs dry with paper towels, as if you're drying a baby after a bath—the goal is to absorb as much moisture as possible. Dry skin is the secret to crisp skin!

Put the chicken on a rimmed baking sheet. Season it on both sides with salt, and don't be skimpy, using 2 to 3 teaspoons (7 to 10 g) of salt total. Leave the chicken on the counter for 15 to 30 minutes, or place it in the refrigerator overnight, lightly covered with plastic wrap.

Sprinkle the skin side of the chicken with the flour. Place a large (12-inch [31-cm]) skillet or sauté pan with 3-inch (8-cm) sides over medium-high heat. Let the pan get hot for 1 or 2 minutes. Pour in the oil—it should immediately start to shimmer.

Put the chicken in the pan, skin side down. Arrange the cloves of garlic around the chicken. Cook the chicken undisturbed for 10 minutes, lowering the heat, if necessary, so that the chicken doesn't burn, until the skin is a rich golden-brown color. Turn the chicken and cook the other side for 2 minutes. Remove the chicken to a plate and pour out all but about a teaspoon of oil.

Pour in the wine and scrape the brown bits on the bottom of the pan. Add the shallots, broth and mustard and stir. Return the chicken to the pan, skin side up. Top with the thyme sprigs. Lower the heat to a gentle simmer, cover the pan and cook the chicken for 25 minutes, until the chicken is tender when prodded with a fork. Remove the thyme sprigs.

Grind black pepper to taste over the chicken and sprinkle it with the thyme leaves. Serve with the pan sauce spooned around the chicken.

PASTA:
FROM
EVERYDAY
TO
ELEVATED

PASTA IS THE CATEGORY THAT DEFINES what family-style dining is all about. Seriously, what could be more crowd-pleasing than bringing out a steaming-hot pasta dish at mealtime and setting it down in the center of the table?

Hands down, pasta of any shape or size is what my family loves best—especially if it's my Family-Style Spaghetti Carbonara (page 100)! And I am not shy about saying it's my favorite food to eat.

I was fortunate to grow up in a family that sat down to old-school Italian-American Sunday dinners. I took it for granted that pasta—or macaroni, as my family called it—would always be there, tossed in a dark red sauce that had simmered for hours on the stove. That gravy, as we called it, was often made with my grandfather's homemade sausage, slow-cooked pork or beef. Of course, Mom's Classic Italian Meatballs with Simple Red Sauce (page 38) made frequent appearances as well.

Homey pasta meals always feel soulful and comforting, but I also love to feature pasta in less-traditional preparations that put vegetables in the spotlight, like Ravioli with Roasted Butternut Squash and Sage (page 111) and Pasta with Broccoli Parmesan Sauce (page 103).

BAKED SHELLS WITH RICOTTA AND GREENS

Kosher salt

1 lb (455 g) Swiss chard

1 (12-oz [340-g]) package dried jumbo pasta shells

2 tbsp (30 ml) extra virgin olive oil

1¼ cups (300 ml) heavy cream

2 tbsp (20 g) finely chopped shallot or red onion

3 cloves garlic, grated on a microplane or finely chopped

½ tsp freshly ground black pepper

¼ tsp freshly grated nutmeg, optional

8 oz (227 g) whole milk ricotta cheese

¾ cup (24 g) freshly grated Parmesan cheese

2 tbsp (4 g) freshly grated Pecorino Romano cheese

FOR A FAMILY-STYLE FEAST

A celebration-worthy menu includes these shells on the table with Mom's Classic Italian Meatballs with Simple Red Sauce (page 38) and a Big Green Salad (page 34).

This cheesy, creamy baked pasta is kind of like my lazy lasagna. It was my mom's baked shells that I looked forward to on holidays and birthdays. But as much as I loved that special dish, now that I'm a mom myself I don't want to spend time stuffing shells. My modern method gives you all the creamy, cheesy delight you could ask for—including those irresistible crusty pasta edges—only with way less fuss. Look for jumbo shells in the pasta aisle of your grocery store. Oh, and be sure to use really good whole-milk ricotta; it's the star of the show here. Go full-fat all the way—you won't be sorry!

SERVES 4-6

Preheat the oven to 400°F (200°C). Bring a large pot of water to a boil and add 3 to 4 tablespoons (30 to 40 g) of salt—you want it to taste salty. Set a colander over a bowl.

Strip off the stems from the chard. Drop the leaves into the boiling water for 30 seconds. Scoop them out with a slotted spoon into the prepared colander. Immediately rinse the chard with cold water and shake a few times to remove excess water.

Gather the leaves into a tight ball, squeezing out as much water as possible. Chop the ball into small pieces.

Cook the shells until they're parboiled (firm in the center and cooked on the surface), 6 to 8 minutes, depending on the size and thickness of your brand of pasta. Drain the shells well in a colander.

Pour the olive oil into a 3-quart (2.8-L) baking dish and swirl it to evenly coat the bottom of the dish. Put the shells and chard in the dish and mix gently with your hands, separating any shells that nest together, until they're coated in the oil and the chard is evenly dispersed.

Whisk the cream, shallot, garlic, pepper and nutmeg, if you like, in a small bowl until everything is blended. Pour the mixture over the shells. Dollop the ricotta by the tablespoon (15 g) over the top of the dish, then sprinkle the Parmesan and Pecorino cheeses over all.

Bake the dish for 25 to 30 minutes, until the edges of some of the shells are golden brown and the whole dish is sizzling. Serve right away, while it's hot.

SKILLET GNOCCHI WITH ITALIAN SAUSAGE AND ARRABBIATA SAUCE

¼ cup (60 ml) extra virgin olive oil, divided

1 lb (455 g) hot or sweet Italian sausage, removed from the casing

¼ cup (60 ml) dry red wine

1 cup (140 g) finely chopped yellow or white onion

1 fresh red chile pepper, chopped

2 cloves garlic, grated on a microplane or finely chopped

1 tsp crushed red pepper

1 (28-oz [794-g]) can crushed tomatoes

1½ cups (360 ml) chicken broth or water

1½ tsp (5 g) kosher salt

1½ lbs (680 g) fresh or vacuum-packed potato gnocchi (not frozen)

½ cup (16 g) freshly grated Pecorino Romano cheese

¼ cup (3 g) fresh basil or Italian parsley leaves

This recipe shows off the true beauty of one-pot pasta. Somehow, the simple combination of ingredients comes together to feel a bit like something you'd order at your favorite neighborhood restaurant. The gnocchi cook right in the pan along with the sauce, an "angry" hot chili-spiced tomato sauce that's a perfect contrast to the soothing, pillowy dumplings. Look for refrigerated fresh gnocchi in your grocery store or use the vacuum-packed shelf-stable variety.

SERVES 4-6

Heat a large (12-inch [31-cm]) sauté pan with 3-inch (8-cm) sides over medium-high heat. Add 2 tablespoons (30 ml) of the olive oil, then crumble the sausage into the pan. Cook until the meat is no longer pink, about 8 minutes. Transfer the sausage to a plate, and pour off the fat from the pan.

Put the pan back over the heat and add the wine, allowing it to bubble and reduce for about a minute while you scrape up any brown bits from the bottom of the pan.

Add the remaining 2 tablespoons (30 ml) of olive oil, onion, chile pepper, garlic and crushed red pepper. Cook for 3 or 4 minutes, stirring, until the mixture softens.

Add the tomatoes, broth and salt and bring the mixture to a simmer. Stir in the reserved sausage and gnocchi, reduce the heat to medium-low and cover the pan. Cook the dish for 8 to 10 minutes, until the gnocchi are tender and the sauce has thickened slightly. Stir everything around once or twice while it cooks so that the gnocchi don't stick to the pan.

Sprinkle the cheese and basil over the top of the pan and serve the dish hot, straight out of the skillet.

FAMILY-STYLE SPAGHETTI CARBONARA

½ lb (230 g) thick-sliced bacon

3 tbsp (30 g) plus ½ tsp kosher salt, divided

3 large egg yolks

1 large whole egg

¼ cup (8 g) freshly grated Parmesan cheese, plus more for serving

¼ cup (8 g) freshly grated Pecorino Romano cheese, plus more for serving

½ tsp freshly ground black pepper

1 lb (455 g) dried spaghetti or linguine

1½ cups (189 g) frozen peas

¼ cup (3 g) fresh Italian parsley leaves, chopped

VARIATION: Sometimes I add a sprinkle of crushed red pepper and ½ cup (44 g) of cooked minced onion to the egg mixture in the mixing bowl. It means there's one more pan to wash, but it adds another layer of flavor.

This book wouldn't be complete without this recipe—it has always been my family's favorite meal. I have variations, and we like it all the different ways. Ever since I discovered how much easier it is to cook bacon on a sheet pan in the oven, I never looked back. This is a meal where a few things are going on at once: water boiling, whisking and tossing. Carbonara needs to be served right away—so call everyone to the kitchen and tell them to get their forks ready!

SERVES 4-6

Preheat the oven to 400°F (200°C), and line a plate with paper towels.

Arrange the bacon on a large rimmed sheet pan. Bake it for 16 to 20 minutes, flipping the pieces over halfway through, until the bacon is deeply colored and crisp. Remove the bacon to the prepared plate to blot excess fat. Chop the bacon into small pieces and set it aside for serving.

While the bacon is in the oven, bring a 4- to 6-quart (3.8- to 5.7-L) pot of water to a boil and add 3 tablespoons (30 g) of the salt.

Put the egg yolks, whole egg, Parmesan cheese, Pecorino cheese, pepper and remaining ½ teaspoon of salt in a large mixing bowl. Whisk together until the mixture is well blended.

Cook the spaghetti until al dente, following the package directions. Scoop ¾ cup (160 ml) of the pasta water out of the pot into a heatproof measuring cup.

Whisk ½ cup (120 ml) of the water into the egg yolk mixture. This tempers the eggs so they won't scramble the sauce.

A minute or two before the pasta is done, dump the peas into the pot. Drain the spaghetti and peas. Immediately transfer them to the mixing bowl with the sauce, then toss quickly and thoroughly, using a pair of tongs, to coat the hot pasta with the sauce. If you think the sauce is too thick, dribble in more pasta water a tablespoon (15 ml) at a time.

Transfer the pasta to a serving bowl, top with the bacon and toss to combine. Sprinkle the carbonara with the parsley and additional grated cheese. Serve hot.

PASTA WITH BROCCOLI PARMESAN SAUCE

3 tbsp (30 g) plus ½ tsp kosher salt, divided

1 lb (455 g) broccoli florets, from about 2 bunches of broccoli

¼ cup (60 ml) extra virgin olive oil

2 tbsp (28 g) finely chopped or grated garlic

½ tsp crushed red pepper

2 anchovy fillets, chopped

1¼ cups (300 ml) water

1 lb (455 g) short dried pasta, such as orecchiette, cavatelli, ziti or shells

2 tbsp (30 g) butter

¼ cup (8 g) freshly grated Parmesan cheese, plus more for serving

Grated zest of 1 lemon

Small handful of fresh Italian parsley leaves

This pasta is over the top. To make it, you must cook the broccoli until it's falling-apart soft so that it literally melts into a creamy, unbelievably tasty sauce. It tastes like the essence of broccoli. I know it goes against our modern sensibilities to cook broccoli until it's way beyond the crisp-tender stage, but trust me on this. It's actually old-school Italian nonna–style. My grandmother never saw a green vegetable that she didn't cook for a looooong time, till it was soft and army-green in color. But whatever overcooked broccoli lacks in the looks department it is worth ten times in flavor. The anchovy is optional if you're vegetarian, but it's in there to add a sneaky, savory layer of deliciousness—that's what anchovies do best!

SERVES 4-6

Bring 4 to 6 quarts (3.8 to 5.7 L) of water to a boil in a large pot. Add the 3 tablespoons (30 g) of salt. Set a colander over a bowl.

Chop the florets and their tender stems into small pieces. Drop them into the boiling water and cook them for 1 minute. Scoop the broccoli out with a slotted spoon and transfer it to the prepared colander to drain. Keep the pot covered on a low boil until you're ready to cook the pasta.

Choose a skillet that's large enough to hold all the pasta and sauce, such as a 12-inch (31-cm) sauté pan. Place the skillet over medium-high heat and add the olive oil, garlic, crushed red pepper and anchovies. Cook for 1 minute, or just until the garlic is fragrant, stirring. Add the broccoli, water and the remaining ½ teaspoon of salt.

Cover the skillet, reduce the heat to medium-low and cook the mixture for 15 to 20 minutes. The broccoli should be soft enough to squish with a spoon.

Meanwhile, cook the pasta until al dente, following the package directions. Scoop ½ cup (120 ml) of the pasta water into a heatproof measuring cup, then drain the pasta in a colander.

Stir ¼ cup (60 ml) of the pasta water and the butter into the broccoli and cook it, uncovered, until the sauce thickens slightly, about 2 minutes.

Add the cooked pasta, and stir until it's coated in the sauce. Dribble in a tablespoon (15 ml) or so more of the pasta water if the sauce looks dry. Add the Parmesan cheese, lemon zest and parsley. Serve with additional Parmesan cheese.

PAPPARDELLE WITH WILD MUSHROOM RAGU

3 tbsp (45 ml) extra virgin olive oil

2 shallots, halved lengthwise and thinly sliced (⅓ cup [35 g])

Kosher salt

12 oz (340 g) portobello mushroom caps (about 6 medium or 3 large) sliced into 2-inch (5-cm) pieces

8 oz (230 g) fresh or dried pappardelle pasta

2 tsp (10 g) finely chopped or grated garlic

2 tsp (2 g) finely chopped fresh rosemary leaves

½ tsp crushed red pepper, plus more to taste

Freshly ground black pepper

2 tbsp (30 g) tomato paste

2 tsp (10 ml) balsamic vinegar

3 tbsp (45 g) unsalted butter

A hunk of Parmesan cheese

Portobello mushrooms are satisfyingly meaty and earthy-tasting, and they match up beautifully with the piney flavor of fresh rosemary. This quick dish is one of the top three recipes on my blog, and it gets rave reviews. The pan sauce delivers the intensely savory flavors of a traditional long-cooked Italian meat sauce—only it's completely vegetarian. Dish it up in bowls with glasses of red wine on the side.

SERVES 4

Put the oil, shallots and a pinch of salt in a large skillet and place it over medium heat. Cook, stirring frequently, for 2 to 3 minutes, until the shallots are softened, but not browned.

Add the mushrooms to the pan. Cook the mushrooms for a few minutes, until they take on some color, then stir and add ½ teaspoon of salt. Continue cooking until the mushrooms become tender and their liquid evaporates, 5 minutes longer.

Meanwhile, bring 4 to 6 quarts (3.8 to 5.7 L) of water to a boil in a large pot and add 3 tablespoons (30 g) of kosher salt. Cook the pasta until al dente, according to the package directions. Scoop out and reserve 1 cup (240 ml) of the pasta water, then drain the pasta.

Add the garlic, rosemary, crushed red pepper, black pepper, tomato paste, vinegar and butter to the mushrooms. Pour in ⅓ cup (80 ml) of the pasta water and stir over medium heat for 1 to 2 minutes, until the mixture becomes saucy.

Add the pasta to the pan and toss it gently with tongs to coat with the sauce, adding more pasta water as necessary (you might not use all the water). Taste for seasoning, and add more salt, crushed red pepper or black pepper to taste.

Shave curls of Parmesan cheese over the pasta with a vegetable peeler and serve.

MIDNIGHT SPAGHETTI WITH CHILI-GARLIC BUTTER

BUTTER

¼ cup (55 g) unsalted butter, softened

2 tbsp (30 ml) extra virgin olive oil

¼ cup (10 g) chopped fresh Italian parsley

2-3 cloves garlic, grated on a microplane or finely chopped

1 tsp crushed red pepper

1 tsp kosher salt

PASTA

3 tbsp (30 g) kosher salt

1 lb (455 g) dried spaghetti

¼ cup (8 g) freshly grated Parmesan cheese

¼ cup (8 g) freshly grated Pecorino Romano cheese

Crushed red pepper, optional

Midnight spaghetti—or *spaghettata di mezzanotte*, as it's known in Italy—is what Italians eat after a night of revelry to cut through the alcohol haze. This pasta contains all the carby, salty, spicy and garlicky deliciousness you crave, regardless of whether you've primed yourself with drink. It's one of those magically quick meals you can turn to whenever you're starving. The butter can be made ahead and will keep for up to a week in the refrigerator. All you have to do is boil the water and get out the bowls and utensils.

SERVES 4-6

For the butter, combine the butter, olive oil, parsley, garlic, crushed red pepper and salt in a mini food processor, or mix it by hand in a small bowl, until the mixture is creamy and well combined, about 1 minute.

Put the butter in a large serving bowl. (If you are making the butter ahead of time, put it in an airtight container and refrigerate it. Remove it from the refrigerator 15 to 20 minutes ahead of use to let it soften.)

For the pasta, bring 4 to 6 quarts (3.8 to 5.7 l) of water to a boil in a large pot, and add the salt. Drop in the spaghetti and cook it, according to package directions, until al dente.

Scoop out some of the pasta water. Add 1 or 2 tablespoons (15 or 30 ml) of the water to the butter and stir until the texture is creamy.

Drain the spaghetti and transfer it to the bowl. Add the Parmesan and Pecorino cheeses. Toss everything together with tongs, coating the spaghetti with the buttery sauce. Serve it sprinkled with additional crushed red pepper, if you like.

RIGATONI WITH WALNUT-PARSLEY PESTO

½ cup (60 g) walnuts

3 tbsp (30 g) kosher salt

1 lb (455 g) dried rigatoni or ziti pasta

⅓ cup (10 g) freshly grated Parmesan cheese, plus more for serving

1 clove garlic, chopped

2 cups (24 g) lightly packed fresh Italian parsley leaves, including tender stems

⅓ cup (80 ml) extra virgin olive oil

½ tsp flaky sea salt, such as Maldon

Crushed red pepper, optional

Making homemade pesto feels like an indulgence at any time of year that isn't summer (i.e., most of the time for most of us). But you can make pesto year-round with Italian parsley, which is always in season at your market. The walnuts add something special to this sauce; to me they taste lightly earthy and savory, and they supply loads more flavor than the traditional pine nuts.

SERVES 4-6

Preheat the oven to 325°F (165°C).

Spread the walnuts on a small baking sheet and toast them in the oven for 15 minutes, until they're just turning golden. Cool them for 10 minutes.

Bring 4 to 6 quarts (3.8 to 5.7 L) of water to a boil in a large pot and add the kosher salt. Drop in the pasta and cook it, according to the package directions, until al dente.

Meanwhile, pulse the cooled walnuts in a small food processor until they look like fine crumbs. Add the ⅓ cup (10 g) of Parmesan cheese, garlic, parsley, olive oil and sea salt, and process until the pesto is smooth, scraping down the bowl once or twice if needed. Scoop out ¼ cup (60 ml) of the pasta water. Stir some of the water into the pesto, a tablespoon (15 ml) at a time, until the texture is saucy like heavy cream—you might not need all the water.

Drain the pasta and transfer it to a serving bowl. Top it with the pesto and toss to coat the pasta. Serve the pasta sprinkled with additional cheese and crushed red pepper, if you like.

RAVIOLI WITH ROASTED BUTTERNUT SQUASH AND SAGE

1 lb (455 g) peeled and seeded butternut squash, cut into 1½-inch (4-cm) cubes

4–5 tbsp (60–80 ml) extra virgin olive oil, divided

1¼ tsp (5 g) kosher salt, divided

Freshly ground black pepper

8–10 fresh sage leaves

3 tbsp (30 g) chopped shallot

2 cloves garlic, thinly sliced

½ tsp crushed red pepper

¾ cup (180 ml) heavy cream

1 lb (455 g) cheese ravioli

2 cups (40 g) baby arugula or spinach greens

¼ cup (8 g) freshly grated Parmesan cheese, plus more for serving

Here, cheese ravioli gets an elegant upgrade! Seek out good store-bought ravioli from an Italian market. The slightly caramelized cubes of roasted butternut squash turn sweet and tender—they're simply delicious paired with the creamy sauce and Parmesan cheese. To save time, look for the packaged butternut squash cubes in the produce section.

SERVES 4-6

Preheat the oven to 425°F (220°C). Toss the squash on a small rimmed baking sheet with 2 tablespoons (30 ml) of the olive oil, ¾ teaspoon of salt and black pepper to taste. Roast the squash for 25 to 30 minutes, until the squash pieces are tender and golden brown in places. Set aside the squash. You can roast the squash up to 3 days ahead.

Bring a large pot of salted water to a boil. Line a plate with a paper towel. Place a 12-inch (31-cm) skillet over medium-high heat for 2 minutes. Add 2 tablespoons (30 ml) of the olive oil and swirl it around the bottom of the pan. Let it heat for about 30 seconds. Add the sage leaves to the hot oil—they should turn bright green, sizzle and pop in the oil. Fry the leaves for 1 minute. Slide them out of the pan onto the prepared plate—a spatula or wooden spoon is a good tool to use for this—leaving the oil in the skillet.

Take the skillet off the heat to cool it down slightly. Return the pan over medium-low heat and add the shallot, garlic and crushed red pepper— add a bit more oil if the pan seems too dry. Cook a minute or two, stirring occasionally, until the garlic is fragrant and the shallot begins to soften. Stir the cream and remaining ½ teaspoon of salt into the shallot mixture. Bring the sauce to a simmer and let it lightly bubble until it starts to thicken slightly, about 2 to 3 minutes.

Meanwhile, add the ravioli to the boiling water and cook them until they begin to bob and float on the surface, about 3 to 4 minutes. Lift them out of the pot with a slotted spoon, and transfer them to the skillet. Use a measuring cup to scoop out ½ cup (120 ml) of the pasta water and add it to the skillet.

Add the roasted squash, arugula and ¼ cup (8 g) of Parmesan cheese to the skillet and stir gently. Turn off the heat when the greens begin to wilt, about 30 seconds. Top with the reserved sage leaves and additional Parmesan cheese and serve.

BEAUTIFUL BOWL MEALS:
SOUPS, STEWS AND GRAINS

ONE DAY, IN FULL MARIE KONDO MODE, I cleared out my kitchen cabinets. Out went many of the plates, and in came bowls of all sizes: deep, shallow and everything in between. Somehow, our eating habits had evolved so that it seemed as though everything I cooked or wanted to eat was served in a bowl.

The organic shape of a bowl is inherently inviting and comforting—they're literally made to be held in your hands. Fill one with warm Cream of Roasted Tomato Soup with Pastina (page 117) and curl up on a comfy chair in front of your favorite movie. You'll feel nourished times ten.

Food served in bowls makes for cozy meals, but it's also the perfect choice when the occasion calls for serving a crowd out of one pot.

The following recipes deliver deep flavors, but they don't take all day to cook. Smoky Chickpea Stew with Couscous and Greens (page 114) and Chicken Posole Verde (page 125), for example, can be ready to enjoy in less than an hour.

SMOKY CHICKPEA STEW WITH COUSCOUS AND GREENS

3 tbsp (45 ml) extra virgin olive oil

1 cup (140 g) chopped red onion

1 jalapeño pepper, chopped

2 cloves garlic, chopped

1 tbsp (6 g) ground cumin

2 tsp (4 g) smoked paprika

¼ tsp cayenne pepper

3 tbsp (45 g) tomato paste

2 (15-oz [425-g]) cans chickpeas, drained

¾ lb (340 g) cooked chorizo sausage (not dry-cured), cut into ½-inch (12-mm) pieces

½ cup (85 g) uncooked pearl couscous

4 cups (960 ml) chicken or vegetable broth

1 tsp kosher salt

1 bunch kale or Swiss chard, stemmed, leaves torn or sliced into bite-size pieces

½ cup (40 g) shredded Manchego cheese

This savory, satisfying stew is one of my favorite things to cook once the weather cools. The best perk: It's a one-bowl dinner, with all your categories covered, from smoky chorizo sausage to tender chickpeas to nutritious leafy greens and satisfying pearl couscous in a spiced-up broth. Make this recipe on busy weeknights or whenever you crave something that's quick and easy but also really delicious.

You can make a meatless version of the stew by substituting an equal amount of vegetarian chorizo. Try Gouda in place of the Manchego cheese.

SERVES 4

Heat the olive oil in a large pot or Dutch oven over medium-high heat. Stir in the onion, jalapeño and garlic. Cook for 3 to 5 minutes, stirring occasionally, until the vegetables are softened.

Add the cumin, paprika, cayenne, tomato paste, chickpeas, chorizo, couscous, broth and salt. Give the mixture a good stir.

Bring the stew to a simmer, then lower the heat to medium-low and partially cover the pan. Cook for 15 to 20 minutes, or until the couscous is swelled and cooked through.

Remove the pan from the heat and toss in the kale, stirring until it wilts into the stew.

Ladle the stew into bowls and sprinkle some Manchego cheese over each serving.

CREAM OF ROASTED TOMATO SOUP WITH PASTINA

3 lbs (1.4 kg) tomatoes on the vine, halved

⅓ cup (80 ml) extra virgin olive oil

1 tsp granulated sugar

2 tsp (7 g) kosher salt, plus more to taste

1 cup (140 g) chopped yellow onion

2 tbsp (28 g) chopped garlic

¼ tsp cayenne pepper

1 cup (240 ml) chicken or vegetable broth

½ cup (120 g) crème fraîche or heavy cream

1 cup (200 g) cooked pastina or other small pasta

Freshly ground black pepper

Freshly grated Parmesan cheese

For a time in my childhood, I subsisted on not much more than buttered egg noodles and Campbell's tomato soup. (I was the "fussy" child.) This is my homemade version, made with roasted fresh tomatoes, and it delivers all the comfort. Make a grilled cheese sandwich on fancy sourdough for dunking into the soup, and celebrate the fact that you're all grown up.

SERVES 4-6

Preheat the oven to 425°F (220°C).

Arrange the tomatoes, cut side up, in a 13 x 9 x 2-inch (33 x 23 x 5-cm) baking dish. Pour the olive oil over the tomatoes and sprinkle them with the sugar and salt.

Roast the tomatoes for 25 minutes. At this point, the tomatoes should be soft and their juices bubbling. Scatter the onion, garlic and cayenne over them and return the pan to the oven for 10 more minutes. Remove the pan from the oven and let the vegetables cool for 10 to 15 minutes.

Transfer the tomatoes in batches to a blender. Purée until they are very smooth, then transfer the mixture to a large saucepan. Stir in the broth and crème fraîche, and heat over medium heat just until the soup simmers.

Stir in the pastina and grind in black pepper to taste. Taste the soup and season with more salt, if it needs some. Ladle the warm soup into bowls and sprinkle it with the Parmesan cheese.

LEEK, POTATO AND MUSHROOM SOUP WITH PESTO TOASTS

2 tbsp (30 g) butter

3 tbsp (45 ml) extra virgin olive oil, divided

2 leeks, white part only, halved lengthwise and sliced

1 cup (140 g) chopped red onion

2 cloves garlic, sliced

1 lb (455 g) Yukon Gold potatoes, cut into ½-inch (1.3-cm) cubes

10 oz (280 g) white button mushrooms, sliced

4 cups (960 ml) chicken or vegetable broth, divided

2 tsp (7 g) kosher salt plus a pinch, divided

1 tbsp (15 ml) fresh lemon juice

2 tsp (2 g) chopped fresh thyme

4 oz (115 g) shiitake or cremini mushrooms, sliced

1 tsp finely chopped or grated garlic

2 tbsp (30 g) crème fraîche or heavy cream, optional

6 slices crusty bread

Walnut-Parsley Pesto (page 108) or prepared pesto sauce

½ cup (6 g) fresh Italian parsley leaves

I'm not one of those people who call a bowl of soup "dinner" . . . unless it's this one. There's enough going on here to make it both satisfying and interesting to eat. It has a dreamy, creamy texture that comes from puréeing some of the soup, so you get the best of both worlds: thick, smooth soup with chunks of mushrooms and potatoes. I add a small amount of crème fraîche at the end, but you can leave it out and it will still be velvety-textured and delicious. Use really good crusty sourdough for the toast, which gets smeared with pesto and dunked into the soup. This a simple, cozy supper perfect for a chilly night.

SERVES 6

Heat the butter and 2 tablespoons (30 ml) of the olive oil in a large pot or Dutch oven over medium-high heat. When the butter melts, stir in the leeks, onion and sliced garlic. Cook for about 5 minutes, until the vegetables soften, stirring occasionally.

Add the potatoes and button mushrooms to the pot. Cook until the mushrooms begin to give up liquid, stirring occasionally, 3 to 5 minutes. Stir in 3 cups (720 ml) of the broth, the 2 teaspoons (7 g) of salt, lemon juice and thyme. Bring the mixture to a simmer, then lower the heat and partially cover the pot. Cook until the potatoes are tender, 15 to 20 minutes.

Meanwhile, heat the remaining tablespoon (15 ml) of olive oil in a medium skillet over medium-high heat. Add the shiitake mushrooms in one layer. Let them cook for about 3 minutes, until they take on some color, then add the pinch of salt and shake or stir the mushrooms around. Continue cooking a minute or two longer, until they're tender. Stir in the chopped garlic, and set aside the skillet.

Scoop 1½ cups (360 ml) of the soup out of the pot, transfer it to a blender and purée until smooth. Pour it back into the pot. You can also use a hand blender right in the pot for this step—just be sure not to make the soup completely smooth. Stir in the crème fraîche, if you like, and remaining 1 cup (240 ml) of broth and heat for a minute or two, until the soup is hot. Toast the bread slices and top each with a generous spoonful of pesto.

Ladle the soup into bowls, topping each with some of the shiitake mushrooms and parsley leaves. Serve the pesto toasts alongside.

CURRY-SPICED RED LENTIL SOUP

CURRY SPICE BLEND

2 tsp (4 g) ground coriander

1 tsp ground cumin

1 tsp paprika

1 tsp ground turmeric

½ tsp freshly ground black pepper

½ tsp cayenne pepper

¼ tsp ground cloves

SOUP

3 tbsp (41 g) ghee, coconut oil or a neutral oil, such as avocado or canola

1 cup (160 g) chopped shallot

1 tbsp (15 g) grated fresh ginger

3 cloves garlic, thinly sliced

2 tbsp (30 g) tomato paste

1¼ cups (250 g) red lentils

2 tsp (7 g) kosher salt

5 cups (1.2 L) vegetable broth or water

1¼ cups (300 ml) canned coconut milk (not light), stirred well to incorporate the creamy top with the watery liquid on the bottom, divided

Black or brown sesame seeds

If you're into one-dish vegetarian meals, this quick soup will warm your heart—just what you'd want for a nourishing supper. Red lentils fall apart into a lovely purée when they're fully cooked, which in my mind is a welcome, comforting texture. Plus, they're ready to eat in less than 30 minutes. Because they're fairly earthy and neutral in flavor, red lentils almost beg to be spiced up.

SERVES 4–6

For the curry spice blend, stir together the coriander, cumin, paprika, turmeric, black pepper, cayenne and cloves in a small bowl.

For the soup, heat the ghee over medium heat in a large saucepan or soup pot. Add the shallot, ginger and garlic and cook for about 5 minutes, stirring occasionally, until the shallot is translucent and softened.

Sprinkle the curry spice blend into the pot and stir to coat it with the oil. Cook for a few seconds, just until it smells fragrant. Add the tomato paste, lentils, salt and broth.

Bring the mixture to a boil, then reduce the heat to a simmer. Cook for 15 to 20 minutes, until the lentils are completely soft and starting to fall apart. Turn off the heat and stir in 1 cup (240 ml) of the coconut milk.

If you enjoy a thick, smooth soup, use an immersion blender to purée most of the soup right in the pot—I prefer to leave a little texture.

Serve the soup in bowls, drizzled with the remaining ¼ cup (60 ml) of coconut milk and sprinkled with the sesame seeds.

FOR A FAMILY-STYLE FEAST

Bowls of this soup go beautifully with a scoop of plain cooked rice and Chili-Garlic Cucumber Salad with Sesame (page 26).

FARRO AND BURRATA WITH BURST TOMATOES

1 pint (300 g) cherry tomatoes, preferably in mixed colors

2 tbsp (30 ml) extra virgin olive oil, plus more for serving

1 tsp plus 1 tbsp (10 g) kosher salt, divided

1¼ cups (250 g) farro

1 tsp red wine or balsamic vinegar

1 loosely-packed cup (12 g) fresh basil leaves

1 (8-oz [230-g]) ball burrata cheese

Here's a simple sorta salad/grain bowl with nutty, whole-grain farro as the base. It's so simple to assemble, and soft, creamy burrata is arguably the best embellishment ever created. In the dead of winter, eating sweet roasted tomatoes is the next best to eating one off the vine on a summer day. This dish is also delicious at room temperature, which means you can pack it up for lunch or pile it into a bowl to share at a potluck. I often make this and leave it on the counter for people to snack on.

SERVES 4-6

Preheat the oven to 425°F (220°C). Put the tomatoes in a medium cast-iron skillet or a heavy ovenproof skillet. Add the olive oil and 1 teaspoon of salt, then give the pan a good shake to coat the tomatoes. Roast for 20 minutes, until the tomatoes have burst.

While the tomatoes are in the oven, bring 3 quarts (2.8 L) of water to a boil in a saucepan. Add the remaining 1 tablespoon (10 g) of salt and the farro. Cook until the grains are tender with a little chew in the center, about 20 minutes. Drain.

Transfer the farro to a serving bowl. Add the vinegar and stir it in. Pour the tomatoes and all their juices over the farro, and sprinkle the basil over it. Tear the burrata into pieces (it will be a bit messy, so do this right over the bowl), and toss everything together gently. Drizzle with more olive oil to taste. Serve warm or at room temperature.

CHICKEN POSOLE VERDE

SALSA VERDE

12 oz (340 g) tomatillos (about 4 medium), husks removed, rinsed and halved

½ red onion, cut into 2-inch (5-cm) chunks

1 jalapeño pepper, quartered

2 whole cloves garlic

2 tbsp (30 ml) extra virgin olive oil

Kosher salt, to taste

2 cups (24 g) fresh cilantro leaves

POSOLE

2 tbsp (30 ml) extra virgin olive oil

1 cup (140 g) chopped red onion

2 cloves garlic, grated

1 jalapeño, chopped

2 tbsp (12 g) ground cumin

1 tsp dried oregano

¼–½ tsp cayenne pepper, to taste

2 lbs (910 g) boneless, skinless chicken thighs, cut into 2-inch (5-cm) chunks

1 (29-oz [822-g]) can white hominy, drained and rinsed

1 (15-oz [425-g]) can white navy beans, drained

2¼ cups (540 g) chicken broth

1½ tsp (5 g) kosher salt

½ cup (120 g) crème fraîche or sour cream

½ cup (60 g) grated Cotija cheese

½ cup (6 g) fresh cilantro leaves

I can hardly find the words to adequately describe how good this stew is—it's hearty and not-too-too spicy, almost like a chili, and makes a perfect one-bowl meal. This dish deserves to be made regularly, once cool-weather appetites set in. Traditional Mexican posole is made with pork, but I make this not-so-authentic version with chicken thighs instead. Hominy is a whole-grain corn that tastes like the essence of maize and smells like a fresh corn tortilla—the tender kernels have a satisfying starchy texture when they're cooked, a delicious textural match with creamy white beans. I highly recommend adding some sliced avocado as a garnish, if you have one or two on hand.

SERVES 6

To make the salsa verde, preheat the broiler to high with the rack placed 6 inches (15 cm) from the heating element.

Put the tomatillos, onion, jalapeño and garlic in a shallow ovenproof skillet (cast-iron is perfect) or on a small rimmed baking sheet. Drizzle with the olive oil and sprinkle lightly with salt.

Broil until the vegetables are sizzling and the tomatillos are softened and browned on the edges, 5 to 8 minutes, depending on the power of your broiler.

Transfer the mixture to a blender and add the cilantro. Purée until smooth; if the mixture seems too thick, add a bit of chicken broth or water to help it blend.

To make the posole, heat the olive oil in a large pot or Dutch oven over medium-high heat.

Add the onion, garlic and jalapeño and cook until the vegetables soften, stirring occasionally, about 5 minutes. Stir in the cumin, oregano and cayenne until the spices are coated with oil.

Add the chicken, hominy, beans, broth, salt and the salsa verde to the pot and stir to combine the ingredients. Bring the mixture to a simmer, then lower the heat to medium and partially cover the pot so that some steam can escape. Cook at a low bubble—not boiling—for 45 minutes. Remove the lid and continue cooking for 10 to 15 more minutes to thicken the liquid slightly; you may need to raise the heat a bit.

Garnish each serving with the crème fraîche, Cotija cheese and cilantro.

VEGETABLES
BY THE
PLATTER

WHEN I GO OUT TO EAT, I nearly always find myself ordering the menu item that comes with the most delicious-sounding vegetables. So it should come as no surprise that the vegetable-based recipes in this chapter are pretty much the foods I most love to eat.

We're talking generous servings of colorful roasted roots, tubers, leafy greens and legumes that will make you want to fill your plate over and over. And what could be better than that?

Casually placed on the table, or kitchen counter, in large bowls or platters, the vegetable dishes on the following pages represent what I consider the single element that brings a whole meal together. Confession: I have a habit of collecting all sorts of platters. Some I pick up for next to nothing at secondhand stores; others are pricier hand-thrown works of art. But all serve as inspiration to cook and share more food with my family.

Please don't think of these as boring "side" dishes. To me, they represent an approach that treats vegetables as stars of the plate in their own right.

I've designed these recipes to match with dishes from the meat and seafood chapters, or to serve in an assortment as a meatless meal. From crusty Olive Oil Smashed Potatoes with Parmesan (page 135) to creamy Italian White Beans and Greens (page 136) to Spiced Roasted Carrots with Pistachios and Labneh (page 143), these are flavor-packed favorites that will have everyone at the table asking for seconds.

GARLICKY GREENS
WITH OLIVE OIL

1½ lbs (680 g) leafy greens, such as kale, Swiss chard or spinach, stemmed, stacked and sliced crosswise into bite-size pieces

3 tbsp (45 ml) extra virgin olive oil

Kosher salt, to taste

2 cloves garlic, sliced razor-thin

½ tsp crushed red pepper

A hunk of Parmesan or Pecorino Romano cheese

If you're as into them as I am, it's almost a daily need to cook a pile of greens, and it's really easy, too. Briefly cooked, wilted leafy greens always have a place on my plate—I love to savor their wholesome taste with nothing more than good olive oil, garlic and a shower of freshly grated cheese.

SERVES 4-6

Place the greens in a colander and rinse them under cold running water, shaking them to drain excess water.

Place a large (12-inch [31-cm]) skillet over medium-high heat. Add the greens to the pan—they should still have some water clinging to their leaves. Cover and cook for a minute or two, just until the leaves turn bright green and begin to wilt.

Add the olive oil and a good pinch of salt, turning the greens with tongs to coat them. Cook for about 30 seconds, then add the garlic and crushed red pepper and cook until the garlic begins to smell fragrant and most of the water has evaporated.

Transfer the greens to a bowl or serving platter. Use a vegetable peeler to shower slivers of Parmesan cheese over the greens, then serve.

FOR A FAMILY-STYLE FEAST

These greens are fantastic alongside any other vegetable in this chapter, and they are especially welcome with meats like 15-Minute Rosemary Pork Chops (page 44) and Herby Spatchcock Chicken (page 55).

ROASTED MEDITERRANEAN VEGETABLES

1 medium eggplant (12–14 oz [340–400 g]), peeled and cut into 2-inch (5-cm) chunks

1 red bell pepper, cut into 2-inch (5-cm) pieces

1 yellow or orange bell pepper, cut into 2-inch (5-cm) pieces

8 oz (230 g) small zucchini, cut into 2-inch (5-cm) pieces

12 oz (340 g) cherry tomatoes, halved if larger than 2 inches (5 cm) in diameter

1 red onion, sliced

2 cloves garlic, grated on a microplane or finely chopped

1½ tsp (5 g) kosher salt

½ tsp crushed red pepper

½ cup (120 ml) extra virgin olive oil

1–2 tsp (5–10 ml) balsamic vinegar

This vibrant jumble of Mediterranean vegetables needs a regular place in your life—I make it all year round to add a taste of summer to the table. Roasting naturally sweet tomatoes and bell peppers makes them taste even more intense, while the eggplant turns soft, creamy and luscious. For this recipe, I choose a good-quality, aged balsamic vinegar for the best flavor. This dish is a great base for a vegetarian supper, spooned over polenta, pasta or simply a pile of greens. I also enjoy the vegetables for lunch in grain bowls using cooked couscous, farro or quinoa.

SERVES 4–6

Preheat the oven to 425°F (220°C), and line a large rimmed baking sheet with parchment paper.

Put the eggplant, red and yellow bell peppers, zucchini, tomatoes, onion and garlic in a large bowl, then add the salt, crushed red pepper and olive oil. Toss with your hands to coat everything evenly.

Dump the veggies onto the sheet pan, and spread them out in an even layer. Roast for 25 to 30 minutes, or until the eggplant is soft and golden brown and the tomatoes are bursting with juice.

Drizzle with the balsamic vinegar and serve.

FOR A FAMILY-STYLE FEAST

Serve the vegetables warm or at room temperature—they are delicious either way. Put them on the table with Super Creamy Homemade Hummus (page 17) and Farro and Burrata with Burst Tomatoes (page 122). Add some crumbled feta, goat or ricotta cheese, if you like.

BROCCOLI RABE WITH CHILI AND PECORINO

2 tbsp (20 g) kosher salt

1 bunch broccoli rabe, trimmed and sliced into large bite-size pieces

3 tbsp (45 ml) extra virgin olive oil

1 clove garlic, thinly sliced

1 tsp crushed red pepper

A hunk of Pecorino Romano cheese

Broccoli rabe, aka rapini, is a leafy vegetable with a unique bitter-green taste. It is a must in our house and has been since I was growing up; I still crave it almost daily. But if you happen to be on the fence about broccoli rabe, I encourage you to try this method of cooking it. Briefly blanching the greens in salted water removes the pungent edge, while preserving a beautiful deep emerald color. The result is tender, almost nutty-tasting greens that need nothing more than a drizzle of your best olive oil, a little garlic, a pinch of crushed red pepper and sharp, salty cheese.

SERVES 4-6

Bring a 3- to 4-quart (2.8- to 3.8-L) pot of water to a boil and stir in the salt. Drop the broccoli rabe into the boiling water and cook it for 1 minute. Drain.

Heat a large skillet over medium-high heat. Add the broccoli rabe in one layer to the pan. Cook until the water clinging to it evaporates, about 1 minute. Add the olive oil, garlic and crushed red pepper and cook the broccoli rabe for another minute or two, tossing it with tongs.

Transfer the broccoli rabe to a platter or bowl, and shave some Pecorino cheese over it with a vegetable peeler.

OLIVE OIL SMASHED POTATOES WITH PARMESAN

¼ cup (40 g) kosher salt

3 lbs (1.4 kg) Yukon Gold potatoes, halved if larger than 3 inches (8 cm) in diameter

½ cup (120 ml) extra virgin olive oil

1 clove garlic, grated on a microplane or finely chopped

½ cup (16 g) freshly grated Parmesan cheese, divided

2 tbsp (6 g) chopped fresh rosemary

Small handful of fresh Italian parsley leaves

Flaky sea salt, such as Maldon

These potatoes are my weakness. You know that saying, "Bet you can't eat just one?" Yep, these are just that addictive—roasted potatoes with caramelized, crusty edges and creamy insides. Bring these potatoes to the table on a large platter or serve them right from the baking sheet. Don't be afraid of the large quantity of salt in the water—that's the true secret to tasty potatoes; the salt seasons them inside and out.

SERVES 6

Bring a 4- to 6-quart (3.8- to 5.7-L) pot of water to a boil and add the kosher salt. Add the potatoes to the boiling water and cook until they're tender, 25 to 30 minutes. Drain.

Preheat the broiler to high, with the rack positioned about 8 inches (20 cm) from the heat source.

Arrange the potatoes on a large rimmed baking sheet. Place another baking sheet on top of them and press down firmly to smash the potatoes. If you don't have a second sheet, just use the bottom of a jar or the palm of your hands to flatten them.

Pour the oil evenly over the potatoes. Slide the sheet pan under the broiler and cook the potatoes for 5 minutes. Rotate the pan and cook 5 more minutes. If the potatoes aren't turning crusty and golden brown, continue broiling another minute or two—timing will vary slightly depending on your oven.

Distribute the garlic and ¼ cup (8 g) of the Parmesan cheese over the potatoes. Broil just until the cheese melts, 1 or 2 minutes.

Transfer the potatoes to a serving platter, and sprinkle them with the rosemary, parsley, sea salt and remaining ¼ cup (8 g) of cheese. Serve hot.

ITALIAN WHITE BEANS AND GREENS

¼ cup (60 ml) extra virgin olive oil, plus more for serving

2 (15-oz [425-g]) cans cannellini beans, drained

3 cloves garlic, grated on a microplane or finely chopped

1 tbsp (3 g) chopped fresh rosemary

1 tsp kosher salt

Freshly ground black pepper, to taste

½ tsp crushed red pepper

¼ cup (60 ml) chicken broth or water

¼ cup (60 g) crème fraîche or (60 ml) heavy cream

Grated zest of 1 lemon

2 generous handfuls baby arugula or kale greens

¼ cup (8 g) freshly grated Parmesan cheese

How delicious are these beans? Let me count the ways. To start, this Tuscan-inspired dish includes aromatic fresh rosemary and lemon. The addition of crème fraîche, Parmesan cheese and a handful of greens means that you can totally get away with calling this a hearty side or vegetarian main. And the creamy, satisfying texture and gentle, earthy flavor of the beans is simply the best. This recipe is a great example of how a can of beans can save the day. When hunger strikes and the cupboard is bare and/or I'm not in the mood for fussing around too much, cannellini beans are winners—they're the ultimate stand-in for comforting carbs, and they're wholesome to boot. I love them!

SERVES 4-6

Place a 10- to 12-inch (25- to 31-cm) skillet over medium-high heat.

Add the ¼ cup (60 ml) of olive oil, beans, garlic, rosemary, salt, black pepper and crushed red pepper. Give the mixture a stir.

Cook for 1 or 2 minutes, until the garlic is fragrant. Add the broth and crème fraîche, and adjust the heat to a gentle simmer. Cook for 5 minutes, stirring once or twice, until the mixture is slightly thickened.

Remove the pan from the heat. Add the lemon zest and arugula, and stir until the greens start to wilt, about 1 minute.

Top the beans and greens with the Parmesan cheese and a good drizzle of olive oil and serve.

FOR A FAMILY-STYLE FEAST

Serve with Herby Spatchcock Chicken (page 55) or Branzino with Fried Lemons (page 73). This dish is also perfect spooned over cooked pasta for the ultimate carb fest.

ROASTED WINTER SQUASH AND SHALLOTS

3 lbs (1.4 kg) acorn, delicata or kabocha winter squash, seeded, peeled, if desired, and cut into 1 x 3-inch (2.5 x 8-cm) pieces

3 or 4 shallots, halved lengthwise and each half quartered in wedges

¼ cup (120 ml) extra virgin olive oil

1 tsp kosher salt

½ cup (6 g) fresh Italian parsley leaves

Crushed red pepper, to taste

When winter squash shows up in farmers' markets and produce stands in the late days of summer, it's a signal to start the inevitable seasonal transition. It can be hard to give up summer tomatoes and corn and make a sharp U-turn toward cool-weather cooking. Thank goodness for all the different colors, shapes and sizes winter squash come in—it keeps things interesting. Because I tend to scoop up different kinds of squash at once, I often make this with a combo of varieties. You don't really need to peel the skin off acorn or delicata squash—it gets tender when cooked, and it helps keep the squash in shape. For a cheffy touch, try drizzling the squash with a tiny bit of aged balsamic vinegar when it comes out of the oven.

SERVES 4-6

Preheat the oven to 425°F (220°C).

Toss the squash and shallots on a large rimmed baking sheet with the olive oil and salt.

Roast for 30 minutes, or until the squash is tender and deep golden brown on the edges.

Scatter the parsley over the vegetables, and sprinkle them with the crushed red pepper to serve.

SWEET POTATO WEDGES WITH MISO BUTTER

2 lbs (910 g) unpeeled sweet potatoes (about 3 or 4 large), halved lengthwise then each half cut into 1-inch (2.5-cm) wedges

3 tbsp (45 ml) extra virgin olive oil

Salt and freshly ground black pepper, to taste

4 tbsp (60 ml) melted butter

2 tbsp (36 g) white miso paste

1 tbsp (15 ml) fresh lemon or lime juice

2 tbsp (6 g) chopped fresh Italian parsley

Crushed red pepper, to taste

It might seem like an odd combination, but sweet potatoes are marvelous with miso paste and (of course) lots of butter. Put the two together—salty, tangy and slightly funky miso and sweet, creamy butter—and you've created a simple finishing touch that turns your ordinary roasted sweet potato into, "OMG, that's amazing!"

SERVES 4-6

Arrange a rack in the lower third of the oven, and preheat the oven to 425°F (220°C).

Arrange the sweet potatoes on a large rimmed baking sheet, drizzle them with the oil and season with salt and pepper to taste. Toss them around to coat them with the oil, then turn them cut side down.

Roast the potatoes on the lower oven rack for 30 minutes. Turn the slices so that the other cut side is facing down. Return the pan to the oven and roast for an additional 10 to 12 minutes, until the skin looks crisp in spots and the flesh is golden brown.

While the sweet potatoes are in the oven, whisk the butter with the miso and lemon juice until the mixture is smooth.

Spoon the miso butter over the hot sweet potatoes. Transfer them to a serving platter, using a spatula to scrape up any caramelized bits from the pan.

Sprinkle the sweet potatoes with the parsley and crushed red pepper and serve.

SPICED ROASTED CARROTS WITH PISTACHIOS AND LABNEH

1½ lbs (680 g) carrots, cut into 3-inch (8-cm) pieces; halve thicker pieces, if needed, for uniform size

2 tbsp (30 ml) extra virgin olive oil

½ tsp kosher salt

1 tsp whole cumin seeds

1 tbsp (15 g) butter

Juice of ½ lemon

½ tsp ground paprika

1 clove garlic, grated on a microplane or finely chopped

¼ cup (60 g) labneh (I like Karoun), or thick plain yogurt, such as Greek- or Icelandic-style

Small handful of fresh cilantro

2 tbsp (20 g) chopped toasted pistachios (see Note)

Flaky sea salt, such as Maldon

1 tbsp (15 ml) honey

NOTE: To toast pistachios, heat a small heavy pan over medium heat until hot. Add the pistachios, shaking the pan frequently, until the nuts begin to release their fragrance. This should take just a minute or two.

Carrots are long overdue for their "it" moment. Far too often, they're overlooked as ho-hum mainstays of the vegetable bin. Perhaps this simple recipe will give carrots their moment. It pairs the humble carrot with a few of its best partners: crunchy whole cumin seeds, the spark of fresh lemon juice and a big dollop of creamy, tangy labneh—a type of thick yogurt cheese. Everything comes together to make a deeply flavorful dish. You'll never look at a carrot and call it boring again!

SERVES 4-6

Preheat the oven to 450°F (230°C).

Toss the carrots on a large rimmed sheet pan with the olive oil, salt and cumin seeds. Spread the carrots in an even layer, and roast them for about 20 minutes, or until the carrots are tender and golden brown in spots.

Remove the carrots from the oven and add the butter, lemon juice and paprika, stirring the carrots around to mix them with the melting butter and spices.

Stir the garlic into the labneh. Transfer the mixture to a serving platter, using the back of a spoon to swirl it around the platter.

Arrange the carrots over the labneh, scraping all the pan juices over the platter.

Tear the leaves off the cilantro stems and scatter the leaves over and around the carrots. Sprinkle the pistachios and flaky salt over the platter, then drizzle the carrots with the honey.

FOR A FAMILY-STYLE FEAST

I love to serve a variety of vegetables at one time, along with warm flatbread to go with Super Creamy Homemade Hummus (page 17), picking and choosing from each platter to make a meal. These carrots match well with any kind of greens, especially Broccoli Rabe with Chili and Pecorino (page 132) and Garlicky Greens with Olive Oil (page 128).

CREAMY BRAISED LEEKS

4 leeks, root ends and dark green tops trimmed off; remaining part halved lengthwise

3 tbsp (45 ml) extra virgin olive oil

½ tsp kosher salt

¼ cup (60 ml) dry white wine

¼ cup (60 ml) chicken broth or water

¼ cup (60 ml) heavy cream

⅓ cup (10 g) freshly grated Parmesan cheese

2 tbsp (6 g) chopped fresh Italian parsley

I have a feeling you might underestimate this recipe. I get it. While the dish is not exactly screaming, "Look how beautiful I am!" you'll have to trust me when I say that you must try braising leeks in the oven. I truly believe it's how this elegant allium was created to be cooked. The leeks turn out meltingly tender, sweet and so delicious. They're fantastic as a side dish, but also try them in an omelet or as a topping for pizza.

SERVES 4

Preheat the oven to 400°F (200°C).

Rinse the sliced leeks under cold running water to remove any sand that may be hiding in the layers. Peel off and discard one or two of the outer layers, as they can be tough. Slice the leeks into 4-inch (10-cm)-long pieces.

Arrange the leeks in a large ovenproof skillet or cast-iron gratin dish. Drizzle them with the oil, sprinkle them with the salt and place the skillet over medium-high heat. Cook until the leeks start to take on a golden color on one side, about 5 to 7 minutes. Pour in the wine and let it bubble for a minute or two.

Remove the skillet from the heat and add the broth and cream to the pan. Bake the leeks for 25 minutes, until the cream is bubbling and the leeks are tender.

Sprinkle the Parmesan cheese and parsley over the hot leeks and serve.

FOR A FAMILY-STYLE FEAST

Pair them with Pinot Grigio–Braised Chicken Thighs (page 92) and Roasted Winter Squash and Shallots (page 139).

SIMPLE
SWEETS

YOU KNOW THAT TIME TOWARD THE END OF DINNER when everyone is lingering around the table, enjoying the last sips of wine and each other's company?

I love that time.

The conversation, the laughter, the sated feeling of well-being—isn't that why we seek to gather with people in the first place?

When you're not quite ready to let go of that magical moment, the ideal segue is "a little something to take away that full feeling"—as my brother-in-law, one of our family's favorite cooking and eating partners-in-crime aptly puts it.

I'm not the world's biggest fan of sweets, and I'm never one to crave an over-the-top dessert, but a little treat often feels like just the right touch to top off a good meal.

That said, when I've already devoted time to cooking dinner, I tend to gravitate toward desserts that are super simple. My favorites lean toward whatever fruits are in season: Peaches, plums, apples or pears can be poached or roasted. Better yet, slice them, then douse them with honey and spoon the honeyed fruit over a slice of Orange Flower Olive Oil Cake (page 151).

And no home baker should be without a recipe for Rich and Simple Dark Chocolate Cake (page 152)—it makes for a luscious last bite.

THE ONE AND ONLY CHOCOLATE CHIP COOKIE

2 cups (280 g) all-purpose flour

½ cup (75 g) whole wheat flour

1¼ tsp (5 g) baking powder

¾ tsp baking soda

1 tsp fine sea salt

1 cup (220 g, 2 sticks) unsalted butter, at room temperature

1 cup (200 g) packed light brown sugar

½ cup (100 g) granulated sugar

2 large eggs

2 tsp (10 ml) pure vanilla extract

8 oz (230 g) dark chocolate chunks or baking discs

There's something magically simple about a chocolate chip cookie. I mean, is there anyone who doesn't have a cherished memory that involves one? For me, the ideal cookie must possess a texture that falls squarely in that sweet spot between chewy and crisp. This is the recipe that manages to deliver both. Here's something else to love: You can whip up a batch of this dough, then chill it briefly while the oven preheats. *Voilà* . . . (almost) instant gratification! If you don't have whole-wheat flour on hand, substitute another whole-grain flour, such as rye or spelt, or just use the same amount of all-purpose flour. Pile the cookies onto a plate or package some in a waxed paper bag to send home with friends.

MAKES ABOUT 2 DOZEN COOKIES

Whisk the all-purpose flour, whole-wheat flour, baking powder, baking soda and salt in a medium bowl.

Beat the butter, brown sugar and granulated sugar on medium speed in a heavy-duty mixer fitted with the paddle attachment until the mixture is light and fluffy, 3 or 4 minutes.

Add the eggs, one at a time, beating until each one is incorporated. Add the vanilla.

Adjust the mixer to low speed and add the flour mixture in two additions, mixing just until the flour is no longer visible. Add the chocolate and stir until it's evenly dispersed in the dough. Put the bowl in the refrigerator to chill while you preheat the oven, about 15 to 20 minutes.

Position a rack in the center of the oven, and preheat the oven to 350°F (180°C). Line two large, rimmed baking sheets with parchment paper.

Scoop the dough onto the baking sheet in 2-inch (5-cm) balls, leaving about 2 inches (5 cm) of space between them.

Bake the cookies, one sheet at a time, until the centers are puffed and the edges golden brown, 13 to 15 minutes.

Transfer the cookies to a rack to cool.

ORANGE FLOWER
OLIVE OIL CAKE

1 cup plus 2 tbsp (160 g) all-purpose flour

Grated zest of 1 orange, lemon or Meyer lemon

¾ cup (150 g) granulated sugar

1 tsp baking soda

½ tsp kosher salt

1 extra-large egg

¾ cup (180 ml) buttermilk

⅓ cup (80 ml) extra virgin olive oil

1 tsp orange flower water, optional, but nice

Powdered sugar

Optional for serving: fresh berries or sliced fresh stone fruits

Everyone needs a recipe in their back pocket for a great olive oil cake, and this is mine. This cake does it all: It looks elegant on the table, topped with fruit for a dinner party, or simply sliced on the kitchen counter for a treat with your morning beverage. It goes with all kinds of lightly sweetened fresh fruit, all year round. This aromatic cake turns out with a perfectly spongy texture and keeps for days. It might be even better the next day—if it lasts that long. Make this easy cake in no time—you don't even need a mixer.

MAKES ONE 8-INCH [20-CM] CAKE

Position a rack in the center of the oven, and preheat the oven to 325°F (165°C). Lightly oil an 8-inch (20-cm) cake pan and line the bottom with parchment paper.

Whisk the flour, zest, sugar, baking soda and salt together in a medium bowl.

In another bowl, whisk the egg with the buttermilk, olive oil and orange flower water, if using, until everything is combined.

Pour the buttermilk mixture over the flour mixture and stir until they are completely combined. Scrape the batter into the prepared pan with a spatula.

Bake for 30 to 35 minutes, until the cake is golden and the top springs back lightly against your fingertip.

Cool the cake in the pan for 10 minutes. Run a knife around the edge of the pan, then gently invert it onto a rack and carefully pull off the parchment paper. Let the cake cool completely.

Sprinkle the top of the cake with powdered sugar or serve plain, topped with fresh fruit.

RICH AND SIMPLE DARK CHOCOLATE CAKE

4 oz (113 g) bittersweet chocolate, chopped

½ cup (40 g) unsweetened cocoa powder

1 cup (200 g) granulated sugar, divided

½ cup (120 ml) boiling water

1 tbsp (15 ml) cognac or whiskey, optional

3 large eggs, white and yolks separated, divided

2 tsp (10 ml) pure vanilla extract

½ cup (50 g) fine blanched almond flour

¼ tsp kosher salt

Everyone needs an exceptionally good chocolate cake in their recipe "wardrobe"—I'm happy to share mine. I think I've made this foolproof cake hundreds of times over the years. Just like an elegant little black dress, the cake is impeccably party-worthy. But, if you're in more of a sweatpants-on-the-sofa mood, it does the trick just as well. This super-chic cake possesses a deep chocolate flavor and a mousse-like texture. It's lovely when served plain, but go ahead and accessorize it! Try softly whipped cream or a scoop of ice cream—or even a simple dusting of cocoa over the top—to glam it up.

MAKES ONE 8-INCH [20-CM] CAKE

Position a rack in the center of the oven, and preheat it to 350°F (180°C). Lightly oil an 8-inch (20-cm) springform pan and line the bottom with parchment paper.

Combine the chocolate, cocoa and ¾ cup (175 g) of the sugar in a large mixing bowl. Pour the boiling water over the mixture. Let it sit for 30 seconds, then whisk the mixture until the chocolate is melted and the mixture is smooth. Whisk in the cognac, if using, egg yolks, vanilla, almond flour and salt until all is combined. Let the mixture cool for about 10 minutes.

Put the egg whites in the bowl of a heavy-duty mixer fitted with the whisk attachment. Beat on high speed until soft, fluffy peaks form, 3 to 4 minutes. Gradually sprinkle the remaining ¼ cup (50 g) sugar into the whites, beating another minute or two until they look firm but glossy.

Fold about one-quarter of the egg whites into the chocolate mixture to lighten it. Add the remaining whites and fold them until completely blended.

Scrape the batter into the prepared pan. Bake for 30 to 35 minutes, until the top is no longer jiggly. A toothpick inserted into the center will come out with moist crumbs clinging to it—this cake is supposed to be moist, so it won't come out dry. Serve in thin slices. To make it easier to slice the cake, run the blade of a knife under hot water for a minute, then dry it with a towel just before you slice the cake.

RUSTIC LEMON CORNMEAL CAKE

1 cup (165 g) polenta or stone-ground cornmeal

¾ cup (105 g) all-purpose flour

1½ tsp (6 g) baking powder

½ tsp fine sea salt

2 large eggs

2 egg whites (¼ cup [60 ml])

1 cup (200 g) sugar

¼ cup (60 ml) extra virgin olive oil, or a neutral oil, such as avocado or canola

2 tbsp (30 g) butter, softened

½ cup (80 g) whole milk plain yogurt or sour cream

2 tbsp (20 g) grated fresh lemon zest

2 tbsp (30 ml) fresh lemon juice

Powdered sugar, for serving

This moist and lemony tea cake rises to a level of rustic distinction with the crunch of whole-grain cornmeal. Try keeping this cake on the kitchen counter for a day or two—I'm guessing it won't last that long!

MAKES ONE 8-INCH [20-CM] CAKE

Place an oven rack in the center of the oven, and preheat it to 350°F (180°C). Line the bottom of an 8-inch (20-cm) cake pan with parchment paper to fit and lightly brush the bottom and sides of the pan with oil or cooking spray.

Whisk the cornmeal, flour, baking powder and salt in a bowl and set it aside.

Beat the eggs, egg whites and sugar in a heavy-duty stand mixer fitted with the paddle attachment on medium-high speed for 4 to 5 minutes, until pale and creamy. On low speed, mix in the oil, butter, yogurt, lemon zest and lemon juice.

Stir in the cornmeal mixture until it's just blended. Pour the batter into the pan and bake the cake for 35 to 40 minutes, or until the top feels firm, but not hard, and a toothpick inserted into the center of the cake comes out clean.

Cool the cake in the pan for 10 minutes before inverting it onto a rack to cool—run a dull knife around the edge of the pan to loosen it first. Sift powdered sugar over the cake and serve.

The cake keeps well for 2 to 3 days at room temperature, wrapped with plastic.

ACKNOWLEDGMENTS

To say writing and photographing a cookbook has always been on my bucket list is an understatement. As a little girl, I would write and illustrate my own "books" using notebook paper, felt-tip pens and a few staples to hold it all together. Now I've checked that box, and I cannot wait to get started on the next one!

Thank you to the team at Page Street Publishing for seeing this project through and helping me to create a beautiful book—I'm so proud to share *Family Style* with the world.

I'm grateful beyond measure to Marissa Giambelluca of Page Street for reaching out to me with the idea for this cookbook. We saw eye-to-eye on the concept from day one: Big platters of rustic food passed around the table are the reason my blog came to be in the first place. I'm so happy you saw one of my recipes on Pinterest and were inspired to cook.

To my family of recipe testers—Dee, Julie, Karista, Laura, Liza and Scott. Your encouragement and enthusiasm helped me nail down these recipes. Big hugs to you all, and I'm counting the days until we sit down to eat together again!

To the chefs, teachers, food writers and photographers who've mentored me in person and in spirit, whose work has guided and inspired my creative journey to food from day one: Maureen Pothier, Melissa Kelly, Alice Waters, Marcella Hazan, Suzanne Goin, Laura Edwards and Jennifer Silverberg.

To all the readers and friends of Familystyle Food, near and far. Thank you for being my pen pals and cheerleaders over the years. Knowing you're there keeps me motivated to keep on cooking.

To my Aunt Janice and Uncle Jim, for your love and support throughout my life.

Tom, Annabel and Jacob: My world revolves around you. I love nothing more in life than nourishing you every single day. Your constant support and love make me the happiest person on earth.

ABOUT THE AUTHOR

Karen Tedesco is a recipe developer, food photographer and creator of the blog Familystyle Food. She grew up in an Italian-American family, for whom Sunday dinners were the norm, and, to this day, she enjoys nothing more than having family and friends over to gather around the table. A former personal chef, Karen trained professionally in restaurants and has won several national cooking competitions. Karen's recipes have been featured on Food Network, as well as in *Fine Cooking*, *Better Homes and Gardens*, BuzzFeed, The Kitchn and many others. Karen lives outside New York City with her family.

Keep up with Karen at FamilystyleFood.com and on Instagram @familystylefood.

INDEX